BITE-SIZE
PYTHON®

BITE-SIZE
PYTHON®

AN INTRODUCTION TO PYTHON PROGRAMMING

APRIL SPEIGHT

WILEY

Contents

About the Author

April Speight is a Python developer with a passion for helping beginners get started with programming. She believes that by providing programming instruction that is equal parts approachable, relatable, and fun she can truly foster a welcoming learning experience. Considered a true creator at heart, April enjoys programming AI assistants and chat bots, creating experiences with mixed reality, and discovering new ways to teach technical concepts to nontechnical audiences. Curious about what she's currently learning or creating? Follow her on Twitter @VogueandCode.

About the Technical Editor

Kraig Brockschmidt has worked on technical developer content for over 30 years, publishing books, articles, sample code, and documentation for multiple languages and platforms. He currently works on developer documentation at Microsoft, specializing in developing with Python on Microsoft's cloud computing platform, Azure.

Acknowledgments

When I began my journey to learn Python, there were few to no resources available online. The programming books in bookstores were less than beginner friendly. The platforms to which we often refer beginners were either nonexistent or within their infancy stage. In summation, the journey to learning foundational programming concepts included *a lot* of heavy lifting for beginners who did not come from technical academic backgrounds.

Today, as I look at the endless number of resources available both physically and digitally for learners, I can say that I am eternally grateful for each and every content creator who has contributed to such a vast number of resources for learning how to code.

As for the book that you're currently reading, I would be remiss if I did not give thanks to the many individuals involved in creating *Bite-Size Python: An Introduction to Python Programming*. To everyone at Wiley, thank you for contributing to a dream of mine, but most important thank you for the opportunity.

To my acquisitions editor, Devon Lewis, not a moment goes by where I share my publishing journey without mentioning your name. Thank you for watching my YouTube videos and believing in my ability to share my content on a larger scale. Furthermore, thank you for fostering the inclusion of diverse voices in the technical publishing world.

To my technical editor, Kraig Brockschmidt, I'm forever grateful for connecting with you professionally. I knew that I could trust you to

take on a project that meant the world to me after the first time I saw your edits on a research assignment for work.

To my family and friends who have checked in on me, supported me, and promoted the heck out of this book since day one, I appreciate and love each and every one of you.

Finally, to the 2013–2014 IT department at CEA (now CTA), thank you for welcoming me into the tech industry with open arms. If it weren't for you all, who knows where I'd be today. Shell, Sterling, Winson, Jay, Jonathan, Ahmed, Tony, Chris, and Kyle, I'm forever indebted to you all.

What Is Python?

Welcome to the world of Python programming! By opening this book, you've opened your world to infinite possibilities in creating with code. Python is a beginner-friendly programming language, and its structure is often compared to the English language.

So, what can you do with Python? Python can be used to instruct robots how to behave or to give commands to artificial intelligence (AI) assistants. With Python, you can automate everyday processes, such as receiving daily reminders to walk the dog or sending a weekly e-newsletter to the community. You can use it to create a blog, build a social media app like Instagram, or even make your own adventure games. In addition, learning Python is the stepping-stone to exploring advanced concepts in web development, data integration with application programming interfaces (APIs), blockchain technology, data science, and AI (such as computer vision, machine learning, and natural language processing to name a few). The possibilities are endless!

How Is This Book Formatted?

This book was written with the true beginner in mind. Never written a line of code in your life? No problem! This book will get you started with the basics of programming to help you gain a solid foundation for Python.

The chapters in this book are written to build upon each other. If you have never written Python code, consider reading the chapters in this book in the order in which they are presented. The following sections explain what you can expect to find in each chapter.

Syntax

Syntax represents a set of rules to follow when writing code. Whenever syntax is introduced for a new concept, the words you should change are shown in italics.

Code Blocks

Throughout this book, you will be introduced to code examples in a *code block*. Whenever a code block is presented, the code will appear as such:

```
>>> print('Welcome to the world of Python!')
Welcome to the world of Python!
```

You are welcome to copy the code as written in the code block into the code editor to try the examples. In addition, you may also notice that some of the words in the code block are written in color. This is known as *syntax highlighting*. Syntax highlighting is a helpful feature designed to help you keep track of the syntax elements within your code.

Checkpoints

Checkpoints throughout each chapter help you confirm that you understand the material presented and give you the confidence to continue learning. Checkpoints are presented in quiz format and may consist of multiple-choice questions, matching, or fill-in-the-blank questions. You can find all the answers for the checkpoints in the appendix, "Checkpoint Answers."

Projects

As you complete the chapters in this book, you will have the opportunity to practice your skills with a project. Each project requires you to write your own Python program. A *program* is a collection of commands within a file that will be run to complete a task. Projects are designed to enable you to use the knowledge you gained in the current and previous chapters. A detailed walk-through of how to complete each project is provided as well. You can find the code for all project files on the Wiley website at www.wiley.com/go/bitesizepython.

You are encouraged to use the projects in this book to build even greater Python programs. Once you start to develop a better understanding of how to use Python, you will find yourself motivated to build. Use the projects in this book as guidance to help bring your ideas to life!

2

Install Python

So, you're probably saying to yourself, "Python sounds so cool—I'm ready to code!" Before you can do anything with Python on your computer, you must install the latest version of the language. Ready to get started? Let's go!

Download Python

Here are the instructions to download Python depending on your platform.

Windows Platform

If you're using a computer that runs Windows, you can download Python from the Microsoft Store. In the search bar, enter **Python** and select the latest version of the language.

Additional information about the language is provided in the **Overview** section. If you're unsure about whether your computer meets the requirements to install Python, check out the **System Requirements** section. Once you're all set, click the **Get** button to start the download.

After the download is complete, follow the instructions in the installation wizard to install Python. When prompted, be sure to check the box **Add Python 3.7 To PATH** (your version number may differ).

Unix Platform (macOS or Linux)

If you're using a Mac or a computer running Linux, it's likely that your computer already has an outdated version of Python installed. You will run into problems using earlier versions of

Python (Python 2.x or older) while completing the exercises in this book. Therefore, head over to www.python.org to download and install the latest version of the language.

After the download is complete, follow the instructions in the installation wizard to install Python.

Check the Python Version

Now that you've installed Python, you can check the version of the language using the *terminal*. A *terminal* is a program that you can use to communicate with your computer. In the terminal, you enter *commands*, which are instructions for the computer to follow. If the computer doesn't understand a command, it'll respond with an error message.

Windows Platform

On Windows, you can use the *Command Prompt* window (which is a terminal) to check the Python version installed. Search for the Command Prompt app to open the terminal.

At start, the **Command Prompt** window loads with default information. Below the default information, you'll see a line that ends with

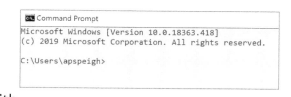

a blinking line. This blinking line, also known as a *text cursor*, is an indicator that the terminal is ready for you to enter a command.

To check the version of Python installed, enter the command **python3 --version** and press Enter.

If the version of Python installed is 3.x or newer, then you're all set to code!

Unix Platform

On a Mac or a computer running Linux, search for *terminal* to open the terminal.

At start, the terminal will load with default information. Below the default information, you'll see a line that ends with a **$** symbol. This symbol, or *text cursor*, is an indicator that the terminal is ready for you to enter a command.

To check the version of Python installed, enter the command **python --version** and press Enter.

If the version of Python installed is 3.x or newer, then you're all set to code!

3

IDLE

When you code in Python, you have to write and run your code in a program that can read and run Python. In the previous chapter, you were introduced to the terminal. Although you could code in the terminal, we'll be using an *integrated development environment* (IDE) instead. An IDE is a powerful program that combines a variety of useful coding tools into a single tool to help you code more efficiently!

Although there are many IDEs on the internet available to download, we'll be using an IDE that comes installed with Python; it is named IDLE.

What Is IDLE?

You can write and run Python code in an IDE that comes installed with Python named *IDLE*. You can use IDLE on both the Windows and Unix platforms as the IDE works mostly the same across each platform.

IDLE is equipped with some useful features to help you out as you code.

- Adds syntax highlighting to your code
- Auto completion
- Multiwindow text editor
- Smart indent
- Call tips
- Command history

These features may not mean much to you now; however, you'll be introduced to the magic of each feature as you read the upcoming chapters of this book.

IDLE Interface

At first look, you may think that IDLE looks like the terminal from the previous chapter. Although you can enter commands into both the terminal and IDLE, there are additional features within the IDLE interface that you'll find helpful as you complete the exercises in this book.

```
Python 3.7.5 Shell                                              —    □    ×
File  Edit  Shell  Debug  Options  Window  Help
Python 3.7.5 (tags/v3.7.5:5c02a39a0b, Oct 15 2019, 01:31:54) [MSC v.1916 64 bit (AMD64)] on win32
Type "help", "copyright", "credits" or "license()" for more information.
>>> |
```

Python Version The version of Python displays at the top of the window in IDLE.

Python Shell Window Here is where you will type, read, and run your Python code. The Python Shell window is also called an *interpreter*.

Text Cursor The text cursor will let you know if it's okay to enter a new command or line of code into the interpreter by blinking repeatedly. If the text cursor isn't blinking, there's a good chance that your computer isn't done completing the command you asked the computer to complete. Just give IDLE a moment to finish completing your prior command before beginning to type.

IDLE Menus There are lots of options available in the IDLE menus. As you work through the exercises in this book, you will notice that the menus in IDLE will change. IDLE has both

a Shell window and an Editor window. Depending on the window type that you're using, the menu options will change.

Run Code in IDLE

Let's take IDLE out for a spin! First, check to make sure that your text cursor is blinking. If your text cursor is blinking, type **print('Hello World!')** into the interpreter and press Enter.

```
>>> print('Hello World!')
Hello World!
```

Congratulations—you just wrote and ran your first line of Python code! So, what exactly happened? The code you entered tells Python to print the text inside the quotes. Try writing another line of code using the same code as before; however, replace Hello World! with another phrase. Be sure to keep the quotes surrounding the phrase; otherwise, the interpreter returns an error after you press Enter.

```
>>> print('Python is awesome!')
Python is awesome!
```

There are two important things to remember about running Python code. First, Python code is run from top to bottom. What this means is that the code that appears at the top of the program is run first and the final line of the code is run last.

Second, Python relies on proper indentation. You will notice later in this book that some of the code examples are indented. Fortunately, IDLE automatically includes indentation for you. However, it's also helpful to be aware of how much you should indent your code when necessary. If you need to manually indent your code, you could use either the space bar or Tab key on your keyboard.

Create and Run Files

Each time you press Enter in IDLE, the interpreter checks if it should run the code. However, this can become unnecessary if you are writing a longer program that contains various logic. Typically, you would create the program, change the logic as you code and then test by running the program. There's little flexibility in changing a piece of the logic if you're creating the entire program in the interpreter.

Fortunately, you can create a file in IDLE that only runs when you ask the program to run. You can edit the program as much as you want and save the program if you would like to access the program later. This is an important difference between coding in the interpreter vs. creating a new file in IDLE that is then ran in the interpreter. Anything entered into the interpreter cannot be saved. Therefore, if you want to create a program that you can come back to later, create a new file in IDLE and save the program before exiting IDLE.

To create a new file in IDLE, click **File** then **New File**. Save the file by clicking **File** then **Save As**. When prompted, save the file to a memorable location on the computer and name the file something related to the program inside the file. Notice that the **Save as type** is Python files. This saves

untitled	
File Edit Format Run Options Window Help	
New File	Ctrl+N
Open...	Ctrl+O
Open Module...	Alt+M
Recent Files	▸
Module Browser	Alt+C
Path Browser	
Save	Ctrl+S
Save As...	Ctrl+Shift+S
Save Copy As...	Alt+Shift+S
Print Window	Ctrl+P
Close	Alt+F4
Exit	Ctrl+Q

the file using the Python extension **.py.** This extension tells the computer that the file is a Python file and therefore the program inside the file only runs using the programming language Python. After you name the file, click **Save**.

To run the program inside a file, click **Run** at the top of the screen and select **Run Module**. Each time you choose to run the module, IDLE checks to ensure that you saved the file. You can use the keyboard shortcut **CTRL+S** or **Command+X** to save the file. Let's practice this setup by creating a new file in IDLE! Create a new file and save as hello_world.py.

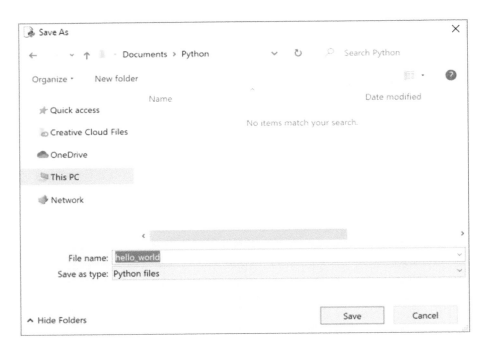

On the first line of the file, enter `print('Hello World!')` and save the file.

```
print('Hello World!')
```

Click **Run** at the top of the screen and select **Run Module**. The original interpreter window that was opened when you started IDLE comes into view and runs the code inside the hello_world.py file.

```
Hello World!
```

If you happen to close the interpreter window, selecting **Run Module** will open a new interpreter window and run the program inside the file.

Each of the projects in this book requires you to create a new file. If you ever get stuck on how to create and run files in IDLE, come back to this chapter for a refresher.

We can do so much more with the interpreter and Python beyond printing phrases. Now that you understand how to write and run Python code in IDLE, get ready to unlock the magic of coding in Python!

Variables

What's your favorite color? If you recall from the previous chapter, you can have IDLE output any phrase you want using `print()`. How about giving that a try now to see your favorite color printed in the interpreter?

```
>>> print('blue')
blue
```

Now, what would you do if you were asked to print your favorite color five times in a row? One option would be to create five `print()` statements that include your favorite color. Although you could do that, after a while you'll start to realize that typing your favorite color over and over again could become pretty tiring, or you may even accidentally spell your favorite color wrong.

Imagine being asked to write your favorite color 20 times or even 100 times! Sure, you could type the same line of code over and over, however, there's a better way to reuse the same word/ phrase in your code.

What Is a Variable?

A *variable* is a name that represents a value, such as a number or piece of text (called a *string*).

variable = value

When you create a variable, you'll want to choose a name that is unique, is specific, is related to what the value represents, and doesn't start with a number or special character. You'll also want to avoid using keywords that already serve a purpose in Python. To review a list of Python keywords, visit `docs.python .org/3/reference/lexical_analysis.html#keywords`.

The variable names shown here are examples of ways that you can name a variable. Some variable names may be just one word, while others may include underscores. You can even create variable names by capitalizing the first letter of each word after the first word, which is known as *camelCasing*.

age   city_names   booksOwned

Once you pick a name for your variable, you can assign a value to the variable such a number or a string. If you're assigning a string to a variable, you'll need to place the string inside quotes—like how you did for printing. You could use either double quotes ("") or single quotes (' '). However, you can't use both.

Thinking back to your favorite color, you could create a variable just for that and assign your favorite color as the value.

```
>>> color = 'blue'
```

If you want to get more specific with your variable name, you could change the variable name to `favorite_color` instead. Whenever you want to create a variable name that has multiple words, you can separate each word with an underscore.

```
>>> favorite_color = 'blue'
```

Now, you've seen how to assign strings to variables, but what about assigning numbers to variables? Almost the same rules apply; however, you don't always need to place quotes around the number. Whether you need to place quotes around a number will depend on what you want to do with the number.

For now, let's start by using the value to print by itself in the interpreter. We can create a variable that represents your age.

```
>>> age = 13
```

So, how can you use a variable? As your coding skills improve, you'll find yourself writing many lines of code all within one program. More often, you'll need to use the same values repeatedly throughout your program. Assigning (or storing) a value to a variable name enables you to reuse the value in multiple places throughout your code. Just be sure to spell the variable name the same way in all places; otherwise, Python will think that you're using a completely different variable.

For example, if you were writing a program that used your favorite color value in multiple places within the code, the variable name could be used in its place to save you both space and sometimes time typing. Therefore, every time you want to refer to your favorite color, you could use the variable `favorite_color`.

 Checkpoint

> **Which of the following variable names cannot be used in Python?**
>
> **A.** mydogsname
> **B.** !_best_friends
> **C.** car
> **D.** vacationCity

Print a Variable

You can ask Python to tell you the value of a variable by using the `print()` statement. Instead of typing a string in the `print()` statement, you would use the variable name in its place and press Enter.

```
>>> print(favorite_color)
blue
```

The interpreter remembers the color that you assigned earlier to the `favorite_color` variable. Want to print your favorite color 20 times or even 100 times? Change your `print()` statement to `print(favorite_color * 20)`. This syntax will multiply the number of times that the variable is printed by 20.

```
>>> print(favorite_color * 20)
blueblueblueblueblueblueblueblueblueblueblueblueblue
blueblueblueblueblueblueblue
```

Printing isn't just for strings; you could also print numbers by using the `print()` statement. Give this a try by printing your age in IDLE.

```
>>> print(age)
13
```

Checkpoint

Naomi is creating a Python program that contains information about her favorite movie. She wants to store the movie title, year of release, rating, and a brief description of the movie. So far, she's created the following variables in her program:

```
movie_title = Toy Story 4
year = 2019
rating = '4/5'
description = 'Woody, Buzz Lightyear, and the rest
of the gang embark on a road trip with Bonnie and a
new toy named Forky. The adventurous journey turns
into an unexpected reunion as a slight detour leads
Woody to his long-lost friend Bo Peep. As Woody and
Bo discuss the old days, they soon start to realize
that they are worlds apart when it comes to what
they want from life as a toy."
```

Naomi wants to print the value of the `movie_title` variable; however, the value assigned needs to be fixed. Which option correctly assigns the movie title *Toy Story 4* to the variable `movie_title`?

A. `movie_title = "Toy Story" 4`
B. `movie_title = "Toy Story 4'`
C. `movie_title = 'Toy Story 4'`
D. `movie_title = 'Toy' 'Story' '4'`

When Naomi tries to print the description variable, she gets an error. What is wrong with the description variable?

A. The variable name is spelled wrong.

B. The string is too long.

C. Nothing is wrong.

D. The string is surrounded by both a single quote and a double quote.

Update Variables

Variables can be used however many times you'd like throughout your code. But what happens if you want to change the value of a variable? By storing a value in a variable, you can update the value in one place. This will become more useful as you begin to write programs with many lines of code!

Let's say that you changed your mind and now you have a new favorite color. You can assign a new color to the `favorite_color` variable, which will change the value stored to `favorite_color`.

```
>>> favorite_color = 'pink'
```

If you were to print `favorite_color`, the most recent assigned value will print in IDLE.

```
>>> print(favorite_color)
pink
```

 Checkpoint

Every year, Harrison travels around the world to visit his friends and experience new cultures. He keeps track of his location in a Python program using the variable `current_location`. He's currently in Italy but travels to New York soon. Since Harrison will be changing locations, he wants to update the `current_location` variable with his destination.

```python
current_location = 'Italy'
current_location = 'New York'
```

If Harrison prints the `current_location` variable, which location will be printed?

A. New York
B. Italy
C. New York and Italy
D. None

Project: Meet Your Classmates

Description:

After a long fun-filled summer break, it's time to return to school! On the first day of school, your teacher asks the class to go around the room and introduce yourselves to each other.

Although you spent time at the pool and on vacation this summer, you also began to learn a new programming language—Python!

Eager to show off your new skills, you decide to create a Python program that enables your classmates to introduce themselves to the class.

Let's get started!

Steps:

Create a New File in IDLE

Before you begin to code, open IDLE and create a new file. Save your new file with the filename **introduce_app.py**. As a reminder, adding the .py extension to the filename lets the computer know that you are creating a Python file.

Decide on Questions

What would you like to know about your new classmates? Think of some questions that may be interesting to you! The example in this book will use these questions:

- What is your name?

- What is your favorite color?

- What is your favorite food?

- What is your favorite TV show?

Print Introduction and Instructions

When the Python program starts, you will want to greet your classmates. To do so, add a `print()` statement to the first line of your program and insert your greeting as a string.

```
print('Welcome back to school! Answer these 3 questions
to introduce yourself!')
```

Be sure to surround the question with quotation marks as shown here.

Create a Variable

You will need to store your classmate's answers into a variable to later print their responses. Let's first create a variable for the question "What is your name?"

We can ask a question and store the answer in a variable using `input()`. When you run your Python program, the question that you place inside `input()` will appear in the interpreter window. A blinking text cursor will appear directly after the question indicating that you need to enter a response.

On the next line of your code, create a variable name and place the question **What is your name ?** inside the parentheses. Be sure to surround the question with quotes since the question is a string.

```
name = input('What is your name? ')
```

Notice how a space is added after the question mark. This will add space between the question and your classmate's answer.

Test Your Code

Whenever you write a new Python program, you will want to test your program along the way to ensure that everything works properly. The sooner you test your code, the easier it will be to spot errors and fix any issues within your program.

Before you run the program, add a `print()` statement on the next line of your code so that the interpreter can print the value of the name variable.

```
print(name)
```

Now, save your program and run it! In the interpreter window, you should be greeted and then asked the question `What is your name?`. Do you see a blinking text cursor next to the question? If so, great! Respond to the question by typing your name and press Enter.

```
Welcome back to school! Answer these 3 questions to
introduce yourself!
What is your name? April
April
```

The program should respond by printing your name! If you received an error while testing your program, check the `introduce_app.py` file to ensure that you typed everything correctly.

Add More Questions

Once you have confirmed that your Python program works well, you can repeat the steps starting at "Create a Variable" to add

the other questions. Here are the questions that will be used for the remaining variables:

- What is your favorite color?
- What is your favorite food?
- What is your favorite TV show?

Be sure to test your program after adding a new question. Once you are done, your code should look like the following:

```python
print('Welcome back to school! Answer these 3 questions
to introduce yourself!')

name = input('What is your name? ')
print(name)

favorite_color = input('What is your favorite color? ')
print(favorite_color)

favorite_food = input('What is your favorite food? ')
print(favorite_food)

favorite_tv_show = input('What is your favorite TV
show? ')
print(favorite_tv_show)
```

Print

Now that all your questions have been added to the Python program, you will need a proper message for your program to use to recite the answers for your classmates. To do so, you can use *string formatting*. You will learn more about string formatting in Chapter 6, "Strings." However, for now, just know that string formatting is a quick way to insert your variable values into a sentence.

f'This is a sentence {variable}.'

Under the final `print()` statement in your Python program, type the following code into your Python program *exactly* the way that it is written here. If you're using your own questions and variables for this project, replace the variable names with your own variables.

```
print(f"Everyone, meet {name}! {name}'s favorite
color is {favorite_color}. {name}'s favorite food
is {favorite_food}. {name}'s favorite TV show is
{favorite_tv_show}.")
```

When you are ready, save and run the Python program. Answer each question that appears on the screen. After you answer the final question, the interpreter window should read something like the following:

```
Welcome back to school! Answer these 3 questions to
introduce yourself!
What is your name? April
April
What is your favorite color? green
green
What is your favorite food? pizza
pizza
What is your favorite TV show? Steven Universe
Steven Universe
```

Everyone, meet April! April's favorite color is green. April's favorite food is pizza. April's favorite TV show is Steven Universe.

If you have made it this far, then congratulations! You just created your first full Python application! Before you close the Python program and share it with others, you may want to go back into the program and add helpful comments that explain the code in addition to commenting out the `print()` statements that were used to test your program. Comments can be created in Python using the # key on your keyboard. Comments in Python are not printed when a Python program is run.

Here is an example of the full program for `introduce_app.py`:

```python
# This app will ask classmates their name and a few
questions about themselves.
# Afterward, the app will share the answers given by
the classmates.

# Greeting
print('Welcome back to school! Answer these 3 questions
to introduce yourself!')

# Question 1
name = input('What is your name? ')
print(name)

# Question 2
favorite_color = input('What is your favorite color? ')
print(favorite_color)

# Question 3
favorite_food = input('What is your favorite food? ')
print(favorite_food)
```

```python
# Question 4
favorite_tv_show = input('What is your favorite TV
show? ')
print(favorite_tv_show)

# Question 5
print(f"Everyone, meet {name}! {name}'s favorite
color is {favorite_color}. {name}'s favorite food
is {favorite_food}. {name}'s favorite TV show is
{favorite_tv_show}.")
```

5

Numbers

Computers, as befits their name, are made to perform calculations or computations with numbers. As a programming language for computers, a core capability of Python is to, well, perform calculations! Python has built-in capabilities that enable the language to perform simple and complex math equations. You may also find other uses for including numbers in your Python program such as collecting

numeric input from a user or relying on a numeric value to determine what action should occur in your program.

Numeric Types

Before you begin using Python to solve math equations, there are two number types that you should know: *int* and *float*.

Int

An `int` (short for *integer*) is a whole number. This means the number never shows a decimal point. Also, integers can be either positive, negative, or zero. Here are some examples of integers:

3200   -84   2   197

Float

A `float` is any number that contains a decimal point. Like integers, floats can also be positive, negative, or zero. Here are some examples of floats:

7.0   9.38   16.001   -35.2

Given any number, the `type()` function tells you whether it's an `int` or a `float`.

type(object)

Let's use the `type()` function in IDLE to see the type of the following numbers:

```
>>>type(37)
<class 'int'>
>>>type(4.2)
<class 'float'>
>>>type(98.321)
<class 'float'>
```

The `type()` function is also useful for identifying the type of any object in Python and will be explored more in later chapters.

You can also change the numeric type of a number by converting a number from one type to another. This process is known as *type conversion*.

int(*float*)

float(*integer*)

To convert an `int` to a `float`, you would pass the `int` value into the parentheses. Likewise, to convert a `float` to an `int`, you would pass the `float` value into the parentheses. Let's see this in action by converting the sum of two floats into an int.

```
>>> sum = 3.4 + 2.7
>>> print(sum)
6.1
>>> type(sum)
<class 'float'>
>>> sum = int(sum)
>>> print(sum)
6
>>> type(sum)
<class 'float'>
```

In the previous example, the variable sum is assigned to 3.4 + 2.7. The sum of the values, 6.1, is of type float because it contains a decimal. Using type conversion, you can reassign the variable to convert the value to be an int. When you now get the type for sum, you can see that sum has been converted to an int. Furthermore, when you print sum, the decimal point, and the values after it are gone!

Arithmetic Operators

Like a calculator, you can use arithmetic operators to calculate values in Python. There's no requirement to convert numbers from one number type to another unless you prefer a specific output for the calculation. Python performs the calculation regardless of the numeric types. However, the result may not be as you intend. Keep these guidelines in mind as you use arithmetic operators in Python.

Any operation with mixed types (int and float) produces a float.

```
>>> type(40 + 2.5)
<class 'float'>
```

Addition, subtraction, or multiplication with int produces an int.

```
>>> type(2 + 2)
<class 'int'>
>>> type(2 - 2)
```

```
<class 'int'>
>>> type(2 * 2)
<class 'int'>
```

Division with an `int` produces a `float`.

```
>>> type(2 / 2)
<class 'float'>
```

Python is pretty smart about using `int` and `float` together! A `float` can always represent anything an `int` can represent—just not the other way around. So, when in doubt, the type goes to `float`, which is why the type for integer division is a `float`.

Order of Operations

Not all equations are created equal! What happens when we try to use multiple numbers and arithmetic operators in one equation? Like algebra, Python also follows the same order of operations known as *PEMDAS*.

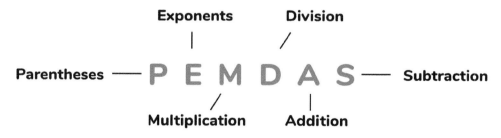

When you ask Python to calculate an equation that contains more than two values, Python refers to PEMDAS to determine which values are calculated first. Python also calculates values from left to right until all that's left is the result of the calculation.

```
>>> 5 * (3**2 + 5) - 8/2
66.0
```

Let's break down the equation completed in the previous example.

1. **Check for Parentheses**   The equation contains only one pair of parentheses. Inside the pair of parentheses is the calculation for (3**2 + 5). Since there are multiple mathematical operators inside the parentheses, Python uses PEMDAS to determine which calculation to solve for first. The ** represents exponent, and therefore Python first calculates 3**2. Python then takes the result 9 and adds that to 5. After Python completes the calculation inside the parentheses, the original equation becomes 5 * (14) - 8/2.

2. **Check for Exponents**   Since there are no remaining exponents in the equation, Python does not perform any more exponential calculations.

3. **Check for Multiplication**   Python now checks for multiplication in the equation. The equation has a calculation for 5 * (14). Python completes this calculation, which changes the equation to 70 - 8/2.

4. **Check for Division**   Looking at what's left of the equation, Python completes the division calculation on the right, 8/2. The equation now becomes 70 - 4.0.

5. **Check for Addition**   Python now checks for addition in the equation. Since there is no addition in the equation, Python does not perform any addition calculation.

6. **Check for Subtraction**   Finally, all that is left in the equation is subtraction. Python subtracts 70 - 4.0, which gives you the result 66.0.

   You can also use variables in place of numbers to perform calculations as well!

```
>>> cakes = 12
>>> pies = 4
>>> desserts = cakes + pies
>>> print(desserts)
16
```

   Try the following checkpoint exercises on paper and compare your answer to the solution by typing the equation into IDLE. The Python syntax for each equation is provided as needed.

Checkpoint

1. $(2 \times 3) + 7^2$
      Python: (2 * 3) + 7**2
2. $72 / 8$
      Python: 72 / 8
3. $3^3 / 2 + 3^2$
      Python: 3**3 / 2 + 3**2
4. $(5 + 10) + (9 \times 5) - 12$
      Python: (5 + 10) + (9 * 5) - 12

Project: Shopping for Science Fair Supplies

Description:

Today in class, Alex's science teacher announced the upcoming science fair. This year, Alex chose to do an experiment on how music affects the growth of plants. After school, her mother took her to the store to buy supplies. However, Alex was given only $25 to complete her experiment. After looking around the store, she found some flowerpots, packs of flower seeds, and bags of soil. Alex wants to use an equation to help her determine the quantity of each supply she could purchase that would be within her budget. The price of each item is as follows:

- Flowerpot: $4

- Pack of flower seeds: $1

- Bag of soil: $5

Create a program using variables and equations that would help Alex determine how much she could purchase for $25. Keep in mind, there is a 6 percent sales tax added to the items in Alex's shopping cart.

Steps:

Open IDLE

Before you begin to code, open IDLE and create a new file. Save your new file with the filename **shopping_cart.py**.

Create Shopping Item Quantity Variables

To give Alex the flexibility of trying different quantities of each item, you can use `input()` and ask Alex to enter the total quantity of the item. Assign the response to a variable that reflects the shopping item. You'll later use the stored values within each variable to calculate the total cost of Alex's shopping cart.

One thing to keep in mind is that Alex's response should be converted to an integer so that the value can be used in calculations with other numeric values that you'll define later in the program. If you don't convert Alex's response to an `int`, the response is the type `str` (which is short for *string*).

```
flowerpot = int(input('How many flowerpots? '))
flower_seeds = int(input('How many packs of flower seeds?
'))
soil = int(input('How many bags of soil? '))
```

Create Shopping Item Price Variables

Next, create variables to represent the cost of each shopping item and assign the cost to the variable.

```
flowerpot_price = 4.00
flower_seeds_price = 1.00
soil_price = 5.00
```

Create Sales Tax Variable

Since a 6 percent tax rate is applied to the items in Alex's cart, you can create a variable for `tax_rate`. To convert the tax rate from a percentage to a decimal, you can divide 6/100, which gives you 0.06.

```
tax_rate = 0.06
```

Calculate Cost of Items

To calculate the cost of the items in Alex's shopping cart, create an equation using the variables created in the prior steps. By adding the value of each variable together, you can get the total cost of the items.

```
cost_of_items = (flowerpot * flowerpot_price) + (flower_
seeds * flower_seeds_price) + (soil * soil_price)
```

You can test the program by printing `cost_of_items`. When you run the program, the interpreter asks you to enter the quantity of flowerpots, flower seed packs, and bags of soil. The program should print the cost of all items.

```
print(cost_of_items)
```

After you test your program, you need to include the tax rate in the calculation to give Alex a total cost after tax. You can take the value of `cost_of_items` and multiply by the `tax_rate`. You can then add that amount to `cost_of_items` to get the total cost of the items in Alex's shopping cart with tax.

```
total_cost = (cost_of_items * tax_rate) + cost_of_items
```

Finally, print the total cost of the items in Alex's shopping cart.

```
print(total_cost)
```

Review the code to ensure that all calculations look correct. Once you're ready, you can save and run the program using different quantities of flowerpots, flower seed packs, and bags of soil.

Here is an example of the full program for
`shopping_cart.py`:

```python
# Ask the user to provide the quantity of the
shopping item
flowerpot = int(input('How many flowerpots?: '))
flower_seeds = int(input('How many packs of flower
seeds?: '))
soil = int(input('How many bags of soil?: '))

# Cost of each shopping item
flowerpot_price = 4.00
flower_seeds_price = 1.00
soil_price = 5.00

# Sales tax
tax_rate = 0.06

# calculate the cost of items
cost_of_items = (flowerpot * flowerpot_price) + (flower_
seeds * flower_seeds_price) + (soil * soil_price)

# Calculate the cost of items plus tax
total_cost = (cost_of_items * tax_rate) + cost_of_items

print(total_cost)
```

6

Strings

Whenever you speak, you use a combination of words to form sentences. If you want to use words and sentences in Python, you'll have to create a *string*. You can use strings as a variable value or use strings to print words or phrases. You can also manipulate strings using Python!

Create a String

A string is a set of characters used for creating words or sentences in Python. A string can be surrounded by either single quotes or double quotes.

'word'

'A sentence.'

You can view how a string looks once your Python program runs by using print().

```
>>> name = 'Monty'
>>> print(name)
Monty
```

If you're typing a long string, it's sometimes best to type the string across multiple lines (also known as *line breaks*) so that the string is easier to read in the program. In IDLE, you can use a triple quote (""") before and after the string to create a string on multiple lines. Press Ctrl+J (Windows) or Control + J (Mac) in IDLE to begin typing on a new line.

```
>>> story = """Once upon a time in
a galaxy far far away was a coder
who loved nothing more than to code in Python!"""
>>> print(story)
Once upon a time in
a galaxy far far away was a coder
who loved nothing more than to code in Python!
```

Escape Characters

If you write a string that includes apostrophes, consider surrounding the string with double quotes. Likewise, if you write a string that includes quotations, consider surrounding the string with single quotes.

```
>>> advice = "You shouldn't eat candy for dinner."
>>> print(advice)
You shouldn't eat candy for dinner.
>>> book = 'My favorite book is "Where the Red Fern
Grows" by Wilson Rawls.'
>>> print(book)
My favorite book is "Where the Red Fern Grows" by
Wilson Rawls.
```

But what happens if you write a string that uses both apostrophes and quotes? Python requires you to use an *escape character*, which enables you to use both apostrophes and quotes in the same string. An escape character is a backslash followed by the character you want to use.

```
>>> feedback = 'The teacher said "You shouldn\'t quit!
Keep trying!"'
>>> print(feedback)
The teacher said "You shouldn't quit! Keep trying!"
```

If part of your string should display on a new line, you can use the \n escape character. This creates a new line in the string.

```
>>> quote = 'Dream it.\nWish it.\nDo it.'
>>> print(quote)
Dream it.
Wish it.
Do it.
```

String Methods

You can automatically change how a string displays when your Python program runs by using a *string method*. String methods are built-in capabilities of string objects to perform string-related manipulations. A string method creates a new value and will never change the original string.

Although there are more than 60 string methods in Python, the string methods covered in this book are useful for completing the upcoming exercises and projects. However, if you would like to review all the Python string methods, visit `docs.python.org/3/library/stdtypes.html#string-methods`.

capitalize()

The `capitalize()` method capitalizes the first character in a string. This is useful for modifying pronouns such as someone's name.

```
>>> name = 'bridget'
>>> print(name.capitalize())
Bridget
```

title()

The `title()` method capitalizes the first character for each word in a string. Consider using this method for books or song titles.

```
>>> book = 'bite-size python'
>>> print(book.title())
Bite-Size Python
```

strip()

Suppose someone provides you with a string that contains a lot of unnecessary characters (such as #, $, %, etc.) or spaces. The strip() method strips away the characters you tell it to get rid of from the string.

```
>>> mood = '!!!happy!!!'
>>> print(mood.strip('!'))
happy
```

If you want to remove extra spaces from the beginning of a string, then leave the parameter empty inside the parentheses.

```
>>> season = '    Summer'
>>> print(season.strip())
Summer
```

lower()

The lower() method turns all characters in a string to lowercase characters.

```
>>> whisper = 'DO YOU WANT TO HEAR A SECRET?'
>>> print(whisper.lower())
do you want to hear a secret?
```

upper()

Likewise, for uppercase characters, you can turn all characters in a string to uppercase characters using the upper() method.

```
>>> yell = "today's the greatest day ever!"
>>> print(yell.upper())
TODAY'S THE GREATEST DAY EVER!
```

replace()

The replace() method takes a chosen character and replaces it with your desired character. The chosen and desired characters are referred to as *arguments*. The first argument will be the character to be replaced, and the second argument will be the character that's doing the replacement.

```
>>> opinion = 'Learning Python is hard!'
>>> print(opinion.replace('hard', 'fun'))
Learning Python is fun!
```

len()

The len() method will count the total number of characters in a string.

```
>>> state = 'Mississippi'
>>> print(len(state))
11
```

 ## Checkpoint

Javier put together a list of his 50 favorite songs of all time. However, he copied and pasted the titles from the internet, which resulted in various title formats. Some titles are in all caps, while some are all lowercase. Javier wants to reformat the list so that the first letter in each word of the song is capitalized. Which string method should Javier use?

A. capitalize()
B. upper()
C. replace()
D. title()

Concatenation

Like adding numbers together, you can also use the + operator to combine strings. Combining strings into one string is known as *concatenation*.

```
>>> animal_first_half = 'mon'
>>> animal_second_half = 'key'
>>> print(animal_first_half + animal_second_half)
monkey
```

Notice how when you combine two strings together, Python does not automatically include a space. To add a space between two strings, add one to the code.

```
>>> summer_hobby = 'I like to go swimming'
>>> winter_hobby = 'and snowboarding.'
>>> print(summer_hobby + ' ' + winter_hobby)
I like to go swimming and snowboarding.
```

Conversion

Python does not allow you to concatenate a string and integer variable together. This is also the case for concatenating a string and float.

Strings have the type str. You can check the type for a string variable using the type() method.'

```
>>> city = 'Los Angeles'
>>> print(type(city))
<class 'str'>
```

In IDLE, check the type for a string variable. Strings have the type `str`. If you try to concatenate a `str` to an `int` variable, Python gives you an error, which states that you can only concatenate `str` to `str`.

```
>>> city = 'Los Angeles'
>>> state = 'CA'
>>> zip_code = 90028
>>> location = city + ',  '   state + ' ' + zip_code
Traceback (most recent call last):
  File "<pyshell#67>", line 1, in <module>
    location = city + ',  '   state + ' ' + zip_code
TypeError: can only concatenate str (not "int") to str
```

However, conversion enables you to change the `int` variable from `int` to `str` so that you can combine the two variables together.

```
>>> city = 'Los Angeles'
>>> state = 'CA'
>>> zip_code = 90028
>>> location = city + ', ' + state + ' ' + str(zip_
code)
>>> print(location)
Los Angeles, CA 90028
```

Calling `str()` on either a `float` or an `int` will change the value to a `str`. However, keep in mind that this change applies only to the output and does not change the type of the original variable.

String Formatting

Let's say you've assigned values to a few variables and would like to use the values of the variables in a new sentence. You

can do so using *format strings* and the f syntax. There are other ways to format strings in Python; however, the f syntax provides the simplest syntax.

f"This is a sentence {variable}."

When formatting a string with the f syntax, you can use either a lowercase *f* or a capital *F*. The f tells Python that the string that follows contains variable references inside curly braces. The variable(s) that you want to embed into your sentence should be an identical match to how you created the variable name(s) in the program.

```
>>> dog_breed = 'poodle'
>>> name = 'Lola'
>>> age = 3
>>> print(f'I have a pet {dog_breed}. Her name is
{name}.
She is {age}.')
I have a pet poodle. Her name is Lola. She is 3.
```

Python automatically converts numbers (int or float) to strings when used in format strings.

Index

In school, you most likely learned to count starting with the number 1. However, Python starts to count with the number 0! Each character in a string is assigned a position or *index*, which indicates the position of the character in the string.

In the previous example, the letter P has an index of 0, and the letter n has an index of 5. Although it may seem obvious to count every character in a string to determine a character's position, Python can save you time with the find( ) method.

variable.find('string')

The find( ) method returns the index of the first time a character appears in a string. You can use the find( ) method to find the index of either a character or a set of characters. If the characters are not in the string, Python will return −1.

```
>>> month = 'January'
>>> print(month.find('u'))
3
```

Using brackets, you can find which character is at a specific index.

variable[index]

```
>>> car = 'Mercedes'
>>> print(car[2])
r
```

You can start counting the index from the end of the string by using a negative value. If a negative value is passed into the brackets, Python starts at the last character, which has an index of −1, and counts backward.

```
>>> car = 'Mercedes'
>>> print(car[-2])
e
```

If returning one character is not enough, you can use slicing to return a range of characters. Slicing enables you to specify two indexes: (1) where to start looking for characters and (2) where to stop looking for characters.

variable[start:stop]

However, slicing can be tricky! Although Python starts at the first index, Python stops at the second index but doesn't include the character at that index.

```
>>> fruit = 'orange'
>>> print(fruit[1:4])
ran
```

To slice all characters after the starting index, leave the second index empty.

```
>>> fruit = 'orange'
>>> print(fruit[2:])
ange
```

Likewise, you could include all characters until the stop index by leaving the first index empty.

```
>>> fruit = 'orange'
>>> print(fruit[:4])
oran
```

Negative numbers could be used as well to count backwards from the end of the string.

```
>>> fruit = 'orange'
>>> print(fruit[:-1])
orang
```

You could also use both positive and negative numbers together. To get all characters between the first and last characters of a string, use [1:-1]. The advantage of using negative indexing in this scenario is that you don't need to know the length of the string to get all characters between the indexes.

```
>>> fruit = 'orange'
>>> print(fruit[1:-1])
rang
```

Project: Mad Libs Generator

Description:

Mad Libs is a game where the reader is asked to provide a series of words that are then used to create a story. The stories are often silly as the reader has no clue how their word choices will be used! Create a Mad Libs generator that prompts you to provide either a noun, an adjective, a verb, or a specific type of word. After you complete all the prompts, the generator uses the words provided to craft a story by inserting the words into a story template.

Steps:

Open IDLE

Before you begin to code, open IDLE and create a new file. Save your new file with the filename **mad_libs.py**.

Create Prompts for Words

A story template for the generator is provided later in this project. You need to enter six different words to complete the story. When the generator starts, you should be prompted to provide each of the six words. Here are the different word types needed:

1. Adjective

2. Name of an outdoor game

3. Adjective

4. Name of friend

5. Verb ending in *ing*

6. Adjective

You can get started by creating variables for each word requested. Notice that the generator needs three different adjectives for the story. Therefore, a separate variable should be created for each adjective. You can prompt a response from the user and store it in a variable using `input()`.

```
adjective1 = input('Enter an adjective: ')
game = input('Enter the name of an outdoor game: ')
adjective2 = input('Enter another adjective: ')
friend = input('Enter the name of a friend: ')
verb = input('Enter a verb ending in ing: ')
adjective3 = input('Enter one more adjective: ')
```

Format the Words

Since there is no logic in the generator that requires you or any other user to enter responses in a certain format, you can use string methods to change how the characters display in the story.

The stored value for *Name of a friend* should have only the first letter capitalized. For all other words, the stored value should be all lowercase.

Change the response for each word using the appropriate string method.

```
adjective1 = input('Enter an adjective: ').lower()
game = input('Enter the name of an outdoor game: ').lower()
adjective2 = input('Enter another adjective: ').lower()
friend = input('Enter the name of a friend: ').capitalize()
verb = input('Enter a verb ending in ing: ').lower()
adjective3 = input('Enter one more adjective: ').lower()
```

You can test the generator to ensure that all works properly by passing each variable into a `print()` statement. Give this a try before moving to the next step.

Create a Story Template

The following story template describes a day at the beach. Copy the story into IDLE and store the template in a `story` variable.

```
story = 'It was a ADJECTIVE 1 summer day at the beach.
My friends and I were in the water playing GAME. As a
ADJECTIVE 2 wave came closer, my friend NAME OF A FRIEND
yelled, "Look! There\'s a jellyfish VERB ENDING IN ING!" As
we got closer, we saw that the jellyfish was indeed VERB
ENDING IN ING! NAME OF A FRIEND ran out of the water and
onto the sand. NAME OF A FRIEND was afraid of VERB ENDING
IN ING jellyfish. The rest of us stayed in the water playing
GAME because VERB ENDING IN ING jellyfish are ADJECTIVE 3.'
```

Using your knowledge of string formatting with the f syntax, replace each of the fully capitalized words with the correct variable.

```
story = (f'It was a {adjective1} summer day at the beach.
My friends and I were in the water playing {game}. As a
{adjective2} wave came closer, my friend {friend} yelled,
"Look! There\'s a jellyfish {verb}!" As we got closer, we
saw that the jellyfish was indeed {verb}! {friend} ran out
of the water and onto the sand. {friend} was afraid of
{verb} jellyfish. The rest of us stayed in the water playing
{game} because {verb} jellyfish are {adjective3}.')
```

Play the Game

It's time to play! Add a print() statement to print the story in the interpreter. Look over your code to ensure that all looks accurate. Once you're ready, save and run the program. You should see a silly story printed in IDLE!

```
Enter an adjective: Lazy
Enter the name of an outdoor game: Tennis
Enter another adjective: Beautiful
Enter the name of a friend: Eric
Enter a verb ending in ing: Singing
Enter one more adjective: Sticky
It was a lazy summer day at the beach. My friends and I
were in the water playing tennis. As a beautiful wave
came closer, my friend Eric yelled, "Look! There's a
jellyfish singing!" As we got closer, we saw that the
jellyfish was indeed singing! Eric ran out of the water
and onto the sand. Eric was afraid of singing jellyfish.
The rest of us stayed in the water playing tennis
because singing jellyfish are sticky.
```

The complete code for this project is shown next. Feel free to get creative and create your own version of the Mad Libs generator!

```python
# Words requested from the user
adjective1 = input('Enter an adjective: ').lower()
game = input('Enter the name of an outdoor game: ').lower()
adjective2 = input('Enter another adjective: ').lower()
friend = input('Enter the name of a friend: ').capitalize()
verb = input('Enter a verb: ').lower()
adjective3 = input('Enter one more adjective: ').lower()

# Story template
story = (f'It was a {adjective1} summer day at the beach.
My friends and I were in the water playing {game}. As a
{adjective2} wave came closer, my friend {friend} yelled,
"Look! There\'s a jellyfish {verb}!" As we got closer, we
saw that the jellyfish was indeed {verb}! {friend} ran out
of the water and onto the sand. {friend} was afraid of
{verb} jellyfish. The rest of us stayed in the water playing
{game} because {verb} jellyfish are {adjective3}.')

print(story)
```

Conditionals and Control Flow

Python can make decisions when executing code based on the logic you add to a script. The logic you add determines what should happen if the code encounters a situation that is either true or false. In Python, the situation is called a *condition*. Your script can contain one or many conditions all with their own set of actions.

Comparison Operators

You may be familiar with comparing numbers in math using phrases such as "greater than," "less than," or even "less than or equal to." Python shares the same comparators with a few additional ones for you to use when comparing numbers or strings. Comparison operators are used to compare two values. When using a comparison operator, Python will return a Boolean value of either `True` or `False`. The return value indicates whether a comparison is true or false. Python will always capitalize the Boolean value.

Operator	Name	Example
==	Equal	5 == 5
!=	Not equal	26 != 3
>	Greater than	100 > 67
<	Less than	89 < 216
>=	Greater than or equal to	90 >= 54
<=	Less than or equal to	23 <= 77

Comparators can also be used for more complex comparisons that involve math equations. Python completes the equation for both sides of the comparator before determining whether the Boolean value is `True` or `False`.

```
>>> 4 * 7 > 98 / 2
```

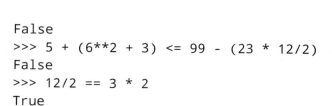
```
False
>>> 5 + (6**2 + 3) <= 99 - (23 * 12/2)
False
>>> 12/2 == 3 * 2
True
```

Strings can also be compared to see whether each value is the same or different.

```
>>> favorite_flower = 'rose'
>>> flower = 'Rose'
>>> print(favorite_flower == flower)
False
```

In the previous example, although both variables are assigned to the same type of flower, the string assigned to favorite_flower is lowercase, while the string assigned to flower starts with a capital R.

Logical Operators

The comparison fun doesn't stop there! There are three logical operators that are used to compare values. Like the previous comparators, logical operators return Boolean values True or False.

Operator	Description	Example
and	Returns True if both statements are true	2 < 3 and 5 > 10 True
or	Returns True if one of the statements is true	1 > 7 or 4 < 3 False

You can use logical operators to evaluate whether two or more expressions are true or not true.

```
>>> (4 > 5) and (3 <= 3)
False
>>> (((20 * 3) + 2) < (100 / 2) * (5**3 - 6)) or ((8 - 7 +1) >= 4)
True
```

In the first example, Python compares the Boolean values for each equation, False and True. The result is False since one of the expressions evaluates to False. In the second example, Python first calculates the total for each equation and compares the Boolean value for each expression, False or False. The result is True since both expressions evaluate to False.

Logical operators are not just limited to comparing numbers. These operators can also be used to compare conditions that consist of strings. For example, you can decide whether to watch cartoons if the day of the week is Tuesday *and* your homework is complete. You can explore this scenario more in the following sections!

if Statements

You can tell your code to take a specific action if all the required conditions are met. Circling back to the example from the previous section, suppose that you can watch cartoons only if the day of the week is Tuesday *and* your homework is complete.

You can use an if statement to determine what will happen in this scenario. An *if statement* evaluates a scenario in this form: if some condition is met, then a specific action will occur.

if some condition:
action

In the case of watching cartoons, *if* your homework is complete, *then* you can watch cartoons. You can turn this conditional logic into an `if` statement in Python. For ease of creating a program for this logic, create a new file in IDLE and save it using the filename **cartoons.py**.

First, create a variable `homework_complete` and set the variable to the Boolean value of `True`. Then, create a variable `day_of_week` and assign the current day of the week to the variable.

```
homework_complete = True
day_of_week = 'Tuesday'
```

Next, create an `if` statement that states what condition must be met for you to watch cartoons. In the `if` statement, include a logical comparator that will compare whether both your homework is complete and the day of the week is Tuesday.

```
if (homework_complete == True) and (day_of_week ==
'Tuesday'):
```

Complete the `if` statement by including a `print()` statement that tells you that you can watch cartoons. Save and run the program to test that your logic is correct. The completed program is provided here:

```
homework_complete = True
day_of_week = 'Tuesday'

if (homework_complete == True) and (day_of_week ==
'Tuesday'):
    print('You can watch cartoons!')
```

if-else Statements

What happens when a condition is not met? Suppose you haven't completed your homework. In the program that you've written so far, there is no logic provided to tell Python what to do if you haven't completed your homework. Therefore, if you change the did_homework assigned value to False, nothing will happen. However, you can provide an action to the if statement using an *if-else statement*.

if some condition:
action
else:
action

An if-else statement first evaluates whether the if condition is met. If the if condition is met, then the first action occurs. However, if the if condition is not met, Python looks at the else condition and takes that action instead.

Update your program to reflect what should happen if you did not complete your homework. After the print() statement, add an else condition and specify what should print if you did not complete your homework.

```
else:
    print("You can't watch cartoons until your homework
is complete!")
```

To test whether your logic works properly, you can change the value assigned to the homework_complete variable to False. After you save and run the program, the string You can't watch cartoons until your homework is complete! should print in the interpreter window.

if-elif-else Statements

But wait—there's more! You may encounter a scenario where the outcome is not as straightforward as an either-or outcome. Since Saturdays are great for relaxing, you're able to watch cartoons even if your homework isn't complete since you have the entire weekend to finish your homework.

You can make your conditional logic more complex by adding even more conditional statements! The `if-elif-else` statement enables you to create multiple conditions for Python to evaluate before taking an action. The *elif* stands for "else if" and is another way of saying "else, do this" or "otherwise, do this."

if some condition:
 action
elif some condition:
 action
else:
 action

Python first starts with the `if` statement to evaluate whether the specified condition has been met. If the condition has not been met, then Python checks the `elif` condition. If the `elif` condition is met, then Python performs the action defined by the `elif` statement and stops evaluating the `if-elif-else` statement. If you find yourself in need of multiple conditions beyond a single `elif` condition, you could add as many `elif` statements as needed. However, the final condition in an `if-elif-else` statement is always an `else` condition.

Modify your program by adding an `elif` statement between the `if` and `else` statements. Like how you formatted the if condition, add a condition for `elif` that checks to see whether the `day_of_week` variable is equal to `Saturday`. If the day is Saturday, use a `print()` statement to give approval to watch cartoons but also remind you to finish your homework by Sunday night.

```
elif day_of_week == 'Saturday':
    print('You can watch cartoons, but you must
complete your homework by Sunday night!')
```

Before you test the program, make sure that the `homework_complete` variable evaluates to `False` and `Saturday` is assigned to the `day_of_week` variable. Save and run the program to check out your logic.

```
homework_complete = True
day_of_week = 'Saturday'

if (homework_complete == True) and (day_of_week ==
'Tuesday'):
    print('You can watch cartoons!')

elif day_of_week == 'Saturday':
    print('You can watch cartoons, but you must
complete your homework by Sunday night!')

else:
    print("You can't watch cartoons until your homework
is complete!")
```

Python first checks whether both the `homework_complete` variable is `True` and the day of the week is `Tuesday`. Since the expressions evaluate to `False`, Python checks the elif condition to see whether the day of the week is `Saturday`. Since `Saturday` is assigned to the `day_of_week` variable, `You can watch cartoons, but you must complete your homework by Sunday night!` is printed.

To test other scenarios, change the program by assigning different days of the week to the `day_of_week` variable and modify whether you completed your homework. Try printing each `print()` statement to the interpreter window! If you're feeling ambitious, add more conditions to the program by adding additional `elif` statements.

Project: What to Wear

Description:

Madison wants to create a program that tells her what she should wear based on the weather conditions.

1. If the temperature is 80 degrees or warmer, then Madison should wear shorts and pack her sunglasses.

2. If the temperature is 60–79 degrees, then Madison should wear a light jacket.

3. If the temperature is 59 degrees or cooler, then Madison should wear a coat in addition to a hat, gloves, and scarf.

Create conditional logic using `if-elif-else` statements to help Madison create her program.

Steps:

Open IDLE

Before you begin to code, open IDLE and create a new file. Save your new file with the filename **what_to_wear.py**.

Understand the Logic

There are three different conditions that Madison wants her program to consider before suggesting what to wear. Each condition contains an `if` statement, an integer, a comparator, and a string. Whether the action (what Madison should wear) is executed is based on the value of the temperature. Therefore, whether a condition is met will be determined by the temperature.

Create a Variable for Temperature

The temperature will vary by day. Therefore, you can have the program ask Madison to provide the current temperature once the program starts. Create a variable `temperature` that prompts Madison to enter the current temperature.

```
temperature = int(input('What is the current
temperature? '))
```

The program will use the value assigned to `temperature` to compare the value to other numeric values. Therefore, make sure that you convert the `temperature` variable to an `int`.

Create an if Statement

Starting with the first condition, create an `if` statement before the variable `advice` that checks whether the temperature is

80 degrees or warmer. If the condition is met, store Madison's outfit suggestion in a variable called `outfit`.

```
if temperature >= 80:
    outfit = 'shorts and pack your sunglasses'
```

You can test the program to check your logic. Add a `print()` statement to the condition that prints the outfit suggestion. When prompted, enter any numeric value 80 degrees or greater. The `advice` string should print with the appropriate outfit suggestion.

Add elif Statements

Now that you've confirmed the initial logic for the program is correct, you can add an `elif` statement for the second condition. Add an `elif` statement to the program that checks whether the current temperature is between 60 and 79 degrees. This logic requires you to compare two expressions using the and logical operator. The first expression will reflect whether `temperature` is less or equal to 79 degrees. The second expression will reflect whether `temperature` is greater than or equal to 60 degrees. If the condition is met, store Madison's outfit suggestion in a variable called `outfit`.

```
elif temperature <= 79 and temperature >= 60:
    outfit = 'a light jacket'
```

You can test the program to check your logic. Add a `print()` statement to the condition that prints the outfit suggestion. When prompted, enter any numeric value between 60 and 79 degrees. The `advice` string should print with the appropriate outfit suggestion.

Add an else statement

There's now just one final condition to add to the program! Since there are no additional conditions, you can create an `else` statement that stores Madison's outfit suggestion to a variable `outfit`.

```
else:
    outfit = 'a coat in addition to a hat, gloves, and scarf'
```

You can test the program to check your logic. Add a `print()` statement to the condition that prints the outfit suggestion. When prompted, enter any numeric value 59 degrees or lower. The `advice` string should print with the appropriate outfit suggestion.

Create a Variable for Advice

Rather than create a separate `print()` statement inside each condition, you can create one that passes the outfit suggestion into a string based on the condition that is being satisfied.

Under the `if-elif-else` statement, create a variable `advice` that uses string formatting to add the `outfit` suggestion to the string `Today you should wear`. Finally, add a `print()` statement to print `advice`.

```
advice = (f'Today you should wear {outfit}.')
```

Before you test the program, comment out any `print()` statements within each condition. Now, save and run the program to test each condition!

If you're up to the challenge, feel free to add more conditional logic to the program. The full program is available here:

```python
# Ask the user to enter the current temperature
temperature = int(input('What is the current temperature? '))

# Compares the current temperature to provide outfit
suggestions
if temperature >= 80:
    outfit = 'shorts and pack your sunglasses'
elif temperature <= 79 and temperature >= 60:
    outfit = 'a light jacket'
else:
    outfit = 'a coat in addition to a hat, gloves, and scarf'

# Advice for the user
advice = (f'Today you should wear {outfit}.')

print(advice)
```

8

Lists

If you were asked to list all your friends in Python, you might think to create a variable for each friend and assign their name to the variable. However, you wouldn't be able to work with all friend variables easily in a program as you would have to remember the variable name for each individual friend *and* apply changes one by one. Python enables you to group related items together into a *list*, which provides you with a better experience to manipulate the collection of items.

Create a List

A list is a collection of items that are ordered and can be changed. This means that each item in the list has a specific position, and if you'd like to change the items in the list, you can do so. You can also have duplicate items in a list.

my_list = ['list item 1', 'list item 2']

Let's create a list that consists of hobbies! Start with a variable hobbies and place each of your hobbies in the list as a string.

```
>>> hobbies = ['swimming', 'dancing', 'singing']
```

To print the list, use print() and pass in the hobbies variable. Python prints the entire list in order surrounded by brackets.

```
>>> hobbies = ['swimming', 'dancing', 'singing']
>>> print(hobbies)
['swimming', 'dancing', 'singing']
```

▶ Checkpoint

Jared wants to create a list of his favorite superheroes. Which list demonstrates the proper syntax for his list?

A. comic_books = ('Spiderman', 'Wonder Woman', 'Hulk', 'Batman')

B. comic_books = ['Spiderman' + 'Wonder Woman' + 'Hulk' + 'Batman']

C. comic_books = ['Spiderman', 'Wonder Woman', 'Hulk', 'Batman']

D. comic_books = 'Spiderman', 'Wonder Woman', 'Hulk', 'Batman'

List Length

You can create a list with as many list items as you'd like. To determine how many items are in the list, use `len()`.

len(my_list)

Using the `hobbies` list, print the length of the list using `len()`.

```
>>> len(hobbies)
3
```

Check Whether an Item Exists in a List

You can search the items in a list to determine whether an item exists in the list using the `in` keyword. A Boolean value returns with either `True` or `False`.

my_list = ['list item 1', 'list item 2']
'list item 1' in my_list

Using the `in` keyword, check to see whether the item `play basketball` is in the list `hobbies`.

```
>>> 'play basketball' in hobbies
False
```

Since `play basketball` is not in the list `hobbies`, `False` is returned. Now, use the `in` keyword to check whether the item `dancing` is in the list `hobbies`.

```
>>> 'dancing' in hobbies
True
```

Since `dancing` is in the list `hobbies`, `True` is returned. What happens if you change the format of the list item? For example, use the `in` keyword to check whether the item `SINGING` is in the list `hobbies`.

```
>>> 'SINGING' in hobbies
False
```

The value `False` is returned because the list item `singing` is formatted in all lowercase characters in the list `hobbies`, whereas the example uses the string `SINGING`, which is in all uppercase characters.

Get Index of an Item

An *index* is the position of an item in a list. To get an item's index, you can use the `index()` method.

my_list.index('list item')

The first index position is 0. Let's print the index of the `dancing` list item from the `hobbies` list.

```
>>> hobbies.index('dancing')
1
```

Access Items in a List

To access a specific item, you can use the index number of the list item.

my_list [index]

Python finds the list item at the specified index and completes whatever action you provide in the program. Let's print the dancing list item from the hobbies list. The list item dancing has an index of 1 (don't forget that Python starts counting at 0!).

```
>>> hobbies[1]
dancing
```

As you may remember, you can use negative indexing in Python as well, which begins counting positions from the end. To access dancing with a negative index, start counting from the last list item in the list (which is -1) and use the negative index for dancing in a print() statement.

```
>>> hobbies[-2]
dancing
```

▶ Checkpoint

What is the item at index [-2] in the list books?

```
books = ["Charlotte's Web", "Holes",
"Matilda", "A Wrinkle in Time", "Hatchet"]
```

A. Matilda
B. Hatchet
C. Charlotte's Web
D. A Wrinkle in Time

Change List Item Value

Using the index, you can change the item in a list to a new item.

my_list [index] = 'new value'

Using the `hobbies` variable, change the `swimming` variable to **snowboarding**. The list item `swimming` has an index of 0. Use this index to change the item and print the list `hobbies`.

```
>>> hobbies[0] = 'snowboarding'
>>>hobbies
['snowboarding', 'dancing', 'singing']
```

Since lists can be changed, the `swimming` list item no longer appears in the list as it's been replaced with the item `snowboarding`.

Alternatively, you could use the `index()` method to change a list item value. The following is an example of using the `index()` method to change the list item `singing` to `running`:

```
>>> hobbies[hobbies.index('singing')] = 'running'
>>> hobbies
['snowboarding', 'dancing', 'running']
```

Python changes the list item at the index for `singing` to `running`.

Add Item to a List

You can add an item to the end of a list by using `append()`.

my_list.append('list item 3')

Add a new hobby **gaming** to the list `hobbies` and print the list. When you add new list items, the items will always be added to the end of the list if you're using `append()`.

```
>>> hobbies.append('gaming')
>>> hobbies
['snowboarding', 'dancing', 'running', 'gaming']
```

Insert Item to a List

You can insert an item into a list at a specified index using insert().

my_list.insert(1, 'list item 3')

Insert a new hobby **rock climbing** to the list of hobbies after the list item dancing. This requires you to use the index of the item after dancing, which is running. The index() method can be used to get the index. Print the list to see the new hobby inserted into the list.

```
>>> hobbies.insert(hobbies.index('running'), 'rock
climbing')
>>> hobbies ['snowboarding', 'dancing', 'rock climbing',
'running', 'gaming']
```

The item rock climbing becomes the list item at index position 2, which means that running has a new index of 3. You can check this by using the index() method to get the index of running.

```
>>> hobbies.index('running')
3
```

Remove Item from a List

You can remove a specific item from a list using remove().

my_list.remove('list item 1')

Remove the running item from the list by specifying the string in the remove() method. Print the list to see that running is no longer in the list.

```
>>> hobbies.remove('running')
>>> hobbies
['snowboarding', 'dancing', 'rock climbing', 'gaming']
```

Remove Item at a Specified Index

You can remove an item from a list at a specified index using pop(). If you do not provide an index, Python removes the last item in the list.

my_list.pop()

Remove the item that has an index of 1 from the list and print the list.

```
>>> hobbies.pop(1)
'dancing'
>>> hobbies
['snowboarding', 'rock climbing', 'gaming']
```

Empty a List

To empty the entire list so that no items are in the list, use clear().

my_list.clear()

Clear all items from the hobbies list using clear() and print the list to confirm that the list is empty.

```
>>> hobbies.clear()
>>> hobbies
[]
```

You could also empty a list by reassigning the variable hobbies to an empty list.

```
>>> hobbies = []
>>> print(hobbies)
[]
```

> Checkpoint

Claudia's birthday is approaching soon! Her parents asked her to create a list of three presents that she would like to receive for her birthday. Claudia began to put a list together but is having trouble managing the list. The following is Claudia's current list of presents:

```
presents = ['basketball', 'book', 'camera',
'headphones']
```

1. Claudia's list looks to be a bit too long. Which function can she use to get the length of her list?

   A. `len(presents)`
   B. `total(presents)`
   C. `presents(len)`
   D. `total(presents())`

2. Since Claudia's list is too long, she needs to remove an item from the list `presents`. She has decided to remove the basketball since she already has one from her last birthday. Which function can Claudia use to remove the item she no longer wants?

   A. `remove(presents(('basketball'))`
   B. `presents.delete('basketball')`
   C. `presents.remove('basketball')`
   D. `presents.remove(basketball)`

3. Claudia wants to be specific about the type of camera that she wants for her birthday. Rather than list `camera`, she wants to specify that she wants a Polaroid camera. Which function can Claudia use to change the item `camera` to Polaroid camera?

A. `'camera' = 'Polaroid camera'`

B. `presents[1] = 'Polaroid camera'`

C. `presents('camera') = 'Polaroid camera'`

D. `presents[2] = 'Polaroid camera'`

Concatenate

When you combine or *concatenate* lists, a new list is created that's separate from the initial individual lists.

my_list = ['list item 1', 'list item 2']

my_other_list = ['list item A']

my_new_list = my_list + my_other_list

Use + to concatenate lists and store the list in a new variable.

```
>>> months = ['January', 'February', 'March', 'April']
>>> seasons = ['Autumn', 'Winter', 'Spring', 'Summer']
>>> months_and_seasons = months + seasons
>>> months_and_seasons
['January', 'February', 'March', 'April', 'Autumn',
'Winter', 'Spring', 'Summer']
```

The list items in the new list `months_and_seasons` stay in their original order from the original lists.

Extend

You don't have to create a new list every time you want to join two lists together! You can also add a list to the end of a list using extend( ).

my_list = ['list item', 'list item']
my_other_list = ['list item']
my_list.extend(my_other_list)

Using the individual months and seasons lists from the previous example, add the seasons list to the end of the months list. When you print the months list, the list months is longer and now includes the items from the seasons list.

```
>>> months = ['January', 'February', 'March', 'April']
>>> seasons = ['Autumn', 'Winter', 'Spring', 'Summer']
>>> months.extend(seasons)
>>> months
['January', 'February', 'March', 'April', 'Autumn',
'Winter', 'Spring', 'Summer']
```

Even though you added the items in the seasons list to the months list, the seasons list is unchanged! Check it out for yourself by printing the seasons list.

```
>>> seasons
['Autumn', 'Winter', 'Spring', 'Summer']
```

Slicing

Earlier, you accessed the items in a list using the index of an item. You can also use the index of an item or items to *slice* a list. Slicing a list will return items within a specified range.

Create a new list **rainbow** and store a list of rainbow colors inside the list.

```
>>> rainbow = ['red', 'orange', 'yellow', 'green',
'blue', 'indigo', 'violet']
```

Use `len()` to get the length of the list. The length of the list is needed to help you determine how many items are in the list.

```
>>> len(rainbow)
7
```

Now that you know the length of `rainbow`, use that as guidance when you slice the list.

To return specific items within a range, pass the list and the index of the item(s) into IDLE. The following example returns the second, third, and fourth items in `rainbow`:

```
>>> rainbow[1:4]
['orange', 'yellow', 'green']
```

Remember that in Python, a range will start at the first index you specify and end before the last index you specify. Therefore, the range in the previous example starts at index 1 of the second item `orange` and ends at the index 4 of the fifth item so that the fourth item green is printed.

You can also use slicing to return all list items before or after an index. To do so, leave either the first index or the second index blank.

```
>>> rainbow[3:]
['green', 'blue', 'indigo', 'violet']
>>> rainbow[:5]
['red', 'orange', 'yellow', 'green', 'blue']
```

In the first example, all items starting at index 3 are printed. In the second example, all items before the item at index 5 are printed.

Negative indexes can be used as well when slicing lists! Python starts at the last item in the list and works backward to return the specified items.

```
>>> rainbow[-5:-2]
['yellow', 'green', 'blue']
```

In the example, Python prints the list items starting at index -5 up to and excluding the item at index -2.

 # Checkpoint

Raul's dog recently had puppies! Before the puppies were born, he decided to let his friends adopt the puppies on a first-come first-served basis. Prior to the puppies' birth, Raul created a list to collect the names of his friends who were interested in adopting a puppy. Now that the puppies are born, Raul realizes that there are 12 people on the list and only 7 puppies. Print a list of the friends in adoption_interest who will be able to adopt a puppy.

```
adoption_interest = ['Mya', 'Shawn',
'Carlos', 'Riley', 'Ashanti', 'Bruce',
'Lauren', 'Mike', 'Keith', 'Kai',
'Shanice', 'Noland']
```

A. adoption_interest[:-4]
B. adoption_interest[1:7]
C. adoption_interest[7:]
D. adoption_interest[:7]

9

for Loops

Computers are great for doing the same thing over and over again, which is mindlessly tedious for human beings. That's a big reason why we like using computers so much! In computer programming, a *loop* is used to create a repeated action, and one such loop is the *for loop*.

Create a for Loop

Suppose you want to print out each letter in the string Python. You could start by creating a variable and assigning the string Python to the variable. Using print(), you could then print the variable. However, look at what happens when you follow those steps:

```
>>> language = 'Python'
>>> print(language)
Python
```

Although the string Python is printed to the console, the goal is to print each letter in the string one by one. To do so, you can use a for loop.

for *item* in object:
action

A for loop repeats the same steps in your code. The process of repeating is called *iterating*.

Iterate over a String

When you create a for loop with a string, Python loops through each item in the string. Within the loop, you can specify an action to take on each item. Let's see this in action with the string Python!

Since you previously created a language variable that stores the string Python, use that variable to create a for loop. First, create a for statement that states "for each item in the variable language."

```
>>> for item in language:
```

You can name the item whatever you'd like. However, consider choosing an item name that relates to the variable.

Now, add an action that you want the program to take for each `item` in the string `Python`. Circling back to the initial goal, print each letter (or *item*) in the string `Python`. In IDLE, press Enter twice after typing the **print()** statement to run the code.

```
>>> for item in language:
        print(item)
```

```
P
y
t
h
o
n
```

The code starts at the first item in the string `Python` and completes the action, which is to print the item. The loop then repeats the same action for the next item in `Python`. The loop continues to repeat until all items in the string `Python` are printed.

Iterate over a List

Iterating isn't just limited to strings. You can also iterate over lists to take an action on each item in a list. Create a list called `continents` that stores a list of the continents on Earth.

```
>>> continents = ['Asia', 'Africa', 'North America',
    'South America', 'Antarctica', 'Europe', 'Australia']
```

Using a `for` loop, print each item in continents so that each item prints individually.

```
>>> for continent in continents:
        print(continent)


Asia
Africa
North America
South America
Antarctica
Europe
Australia
```

The loop starts with the first item, Asia, and prints the value to the interpreter. The loop then repeats and prints the next continent. This process continues until all items in the list continents are printed.

Create a break Statement

To stop a loop, you can add a *break statement* to the loop. A break statement stops the loop from iterating before the loop has looped through all the items.

for item in object:
action
break

An if statement helps the loop determine whether it should break. If the condition in the if statement is met, the loop will stop iterating. However, if the condition in the if statement hasn't been met, the loop will continue until the condition is met.

To see this in action, print all items in the list `continents` up to and including `Antarctica`. Re-create the `for` loop from the prior example including the `print()` statement that prints the item. Add an `if` statement inside the `for` loop that checks whether the next item printed is equal to the string `Antarctica`.

```
>>> for continent in continents:
        print(continent)
        if continent == 'Antarctica':
            break


Asia
Africa
North America
South America
Antarctica
```

Python starts with the first item, `Asia`, and prints the item to the interpreter. Python then checks whether the current item in the loop is equal to the string `Antarctica`. Since the string `Asia` is not equal to `Antarctica`, Python continues to loop through the list `continents` until the item is equal to `Antarctica`. Once Python reaches the item `Antarctica`, Python prints the item and sees that the item string is indeed equal to `Antarctica`. The loop breaks, and the remaining items in the list `continents` are not looped nor printed.

Create a continue Statement

But what should you do if you want your loop to break the current looping and pick things back up at a new point? You can use a `continue` statement to tell the loop to stop looping and then continue to loop after a specified condition.

for *item* in object:
action
continue

Try using a continue statement to loop through each item in the list `continents`, stop at `North America`, and continue looping at `South America`, use the magic of an `if` statement and `continue` statement! First, create a `for` loop that sets up the iteration for the items in the list `continents`. Add an `if` statement that checks whether the item is equal to the string `North America`. If the item is equal to `North America`, the loop should continue. Otherwise, the `for` loop should print the item.

```
>>> for continent in continents:
        if continent == 'North America':
            continue
        print(continent)


Asia
Africa
South America
Antarctica
Europe
Australia
```

Python starts with the first item, `Asia`, and checks whether the item is equal to the string `North America`. Since the string `Asia` does not equal the string `North America`, the item is printed. The loop continues to iterate through the items in the list until the item is equal to the string `North America`. Once the loop gets to the item `North America`, Python sees that the item `North America` is equal to the string `North America`. Therefore, the loop stops and does not complete the `print()` action that follows the `continue` statement. Instead, Python starts the loop again at the next item, South America, and continues the loop until all items in the list `continents` have been iterated over.

 Checkpoint

> There was a glitch in the grading system that decreased the recent test scores stored in Mr. Klein's grade book by three points. Which `for` loop can Mr. Klein use to increase each test score by three points and print the new test score?
>
> **A.**
>
> ```
> >>> for score in test_scores:
>         score = score + 3
>         print score
> ```
>
> **B.**
>
> ```
> >>> for score in test_scores:
>         score += 3
>         print(score)
> ```
>
> **C.**
>
> ```
> >>> for score in test_scores:
>         score * 3
>         print(score)
> ```
>
> **D.**
>
> ```
> >>> for score in test_scores:
>         score += 3
>         print ('score')
> ```

Use range()

Oftentimes, you want to iterate some number of times using numbers in a range. The range() function gives you a way to create a list of numbers that you can use in a for loop.

for *item* in range(*int*):
action

The range() function includes *start* and *stop* parameters that specify where the range should begin and end. The default start parameter is 0. However, if you want a specific range, you need to use the start, stop syntax.

Let's first create a range using the default start parameter. Python can print a sequence of numbers from 0 through 10 using a for loop and range(). Specify the number that the range should count to (but not include) inside the parentheses.

```
>>> for x in range(11):
        print(x)


0
1
2
3
4
5
6
7
8
9
10
```

Python starts with 0 and prints the value. Python continues to loop through each item in the range until all numbers 0–10 are printed. Since Python starts counting at 0, only 11 values in total are printed.

To specify a specific range, enter both a start and stop parameter inside range().

for *item* in range(start, stop): action

The first parameter determines where the range should start to count. The second number determines where the counting should stop. Using this syntax, use a for loop and range() to print a sequence of numbers from 3 through 7.

```
>>> for x in range(3,8):
        print(x)


3
4
5
6
7
```

The for loop starts at the number 3 and prints each value up to but not including 8.

You could also get even more creative by telling the code to skip a specific amount of numbers as the code loops through the range. This process of skipping or incrementing can be done with a *step* parameter.

for *item* in range(start, stop, step): action

The first parameter still tells the code where the loop starts, and the second parameter tells the code where the loop stops. However, the third parameter tells the code how much the count should increment (or increase) while the code loops over the range.

Using this syntax, use a for loop and range() to print a sequence of numbers from 10 through 100 incremented by 10.

```
>>> for x in range(10,101,10):
        print(x)


10
20
30
40
50
60
70
80
90
100
```

Since you want the range to count up to and include 100, the stop parameter must be 1 greater than 100. Python starts with the number 10, increases the next value printed by 10, and prints the number. This loop continues until the full range is iterated over.

Project: Find the Green Marble

Description:

Mariah recently started a marble collection that consists of the following marbles and quantities:

- Red: 2
- Orange: 1
- Pink: 3
- Yellow: 2

Unfortunately, Mariah is having trouble finding green marbles to add to her collection. While on summer vacation, she discovered a marble store nearby that lets customers pick marbles to purchase from a secret bag. The catch to picking marbles from the bag is that Mariah is not allowed to look inside the bag, and she can pick only five marbles from the bag per day. If she chooses not to keep a marble that is picked, she must place the marble back into the bag. Since Mariah wants one green marble, she wants to stop picking marbles once a green marble is found.

The secret bag contains the following quantities of marbles:

- Blue: 3
- Green: 4
- Orange: 1
- Purple: 2
- Yellow: 2
- Pink: 2
- Red: 4

Create a program that keeps track of how many times Mariah has picked a marble from the bag and confirms whether the marble picked is green. If Mariah picks a green marble from the bag, add the marble to Mariah's collection and remove the marble from the secret bag. Once Mariah picks a green marble, she should stop picking marbles from the secret bag. Keep in mind that Mariah is only allowed to pick five marbles from the secret bag per day.

Steps:

Open IDLE

Before you begin to code, open IDLE and create a new file. Save your new file with the name **marbles.py**.

Import the Random Module

Python comes equipped with built-in modules that you can use in your programs. Such modules enable you to perform some interesting actions in your code! The *random* module enables you to return random values. Within the random module is a `random.choice()` function that returns a random item from a list. To use a module in Python, you must first import the module.

import module

In IDLE, import the random module so that you can use the `random.choice()` function in your program to pick marbles from the secret bag of marbles.

```
import random
```

Create a List for Mariah's Collection

As Mariah picks marbles from the secret bag, she needs to add any green marble she picks to her collection. Create a list called `collection` for Mariah's current collection of marbles.

```
collection = ['red', 'pink', 'orange', 'red', 'pink',
'yellow', 'pink', 'yellow']
```

Create a Secret Bag

Since you know which marbles are inside the secret bag, create a list called `secret_bag` to keep track of which marbles are available to choose from.

```
secret_bag = ['pink', 'blue', 'green', 'orange', 'red',
'purple', 'green', 'blue', 'blue', 'red', 'green',
'purple', 'yellow', 'red', 'pink', 'red', 'green',
'yellow']
```

The order in which you enter the marbles inside the bag does not matter since Mariah will pick a marble at random.

Create a List for Marbles Chosen

To keep track of which marbles Mariah has picked, you can create an empty list and later add the chosen marbles to the list. To create an empty list, leave the items inside the list empty.

```
marbles_chosen = []
```

Track the Tries Remaining

The marble store has a strict rule for the secret bag! Customers can pick only five marbles from the bag a day. Keep track of the number of picks remaining for Mariah by creating a variable called `tries_remaining`.

```
tries_remaining = 5
```

As Mariah picks a marble from the secret bag, the number of tries remaining will decrease until the total number of tries remaining is 0.

Create a for Loop to Iterate

Since Python cannot iterate over an `int`, you can use `range()` to loop five times and pick a random marble. Keep in mind that when using `range()`, the loop will perform the iteration 1 minus the number passed into the parentheses.

```
for x in range(6):
```

Create Nested if Statements

There are a couple of conditional statements that the program needs to consider before allowing Mariah to pick another marble. In Python, you can use an `if` statement inside another `if` statement. This is known as *nesting*. First, create an `if` statement inside the `for` loop that checks whether the number of tries remaining is greater than 0. If the number of tries remaining is less than 0, print a message that lets Mariah know that she is out of tries and should try again tomorrow.

```
if tries_remaining > 0:
else:
    print('Sorry, you are out of tries. Please come
back tomorrow and try again!')
```

There are a couple of actions that take place if the number of tries is greater than six. Inside the `if` statement but before the `else` statement, select a random marble from the secret bag, add the marble to the list of marbles chosen, and decrease the number of tries remaining. As a reminder, the `random.choice()` function can be used to pick a random item from a list.

```
selection = random.choice(secret_bag)
marbles_chosen.append(selection)
tries_remaining -= 1
```

You can create a variable called `selection` to store the randomly selected marble. The marble stored inside `selection` can then be added to the `marbles_chosen` list that is being used to track the marbles picked from the secret bag. After the marble selected is added to `marbles_chosen`, you can decrease the number of tries remaining by decrementing the value of `tries_remaining` by 1.

Now it's time to nest an `if` statement! After the number of tries remaining is decreased, create an `if` statement that checks whether the marble chosen at random is green. If the random marble is green, add the marble to Mariah's collection and remove the marble from the secret bag.

```
if selection == 'green':
    collection.append(selection)
    secret_bag.remove(selection)
```

In the nested `if` statement, you can check whether the value stored to `selection` is equal to the string green. If the value is equal to green, the value (or marble) is added to Mariah's collection using `append()` and removed from the secret bag using `remove()`.

Let's create one more nested `if` statement! This `if` statement will be used to break the loop once a green marble is added to Mariah's collection. If the loop breaks, print a statement that lets Mariah know that she has picked a green marble. In addition, let Mariah know how many tries she has remaining.

```
if ('green' in collection):
    print(f'Awesome! You found a green marble. If you
would like another marble, you have {tries_remaining}
pick(s) left.')
    break
```

The `in` keyword is used to check whether the item `green` is in the list `collection`. The `print()` statement that follows uses string formatting to pass the value assigned to `tries_remaining` into the printed string. The `break` statement is then used to stop the loop from looping.

Print the Marbles Chosen

To let Mariah know which marbles were chosen up until the loop stopped, write a `print()` statement that uses string formatting and prints the items in the list `marbles_chosen`. The `print()` statement should be outside the `for` loop.

```
print(f'Here are all the marbles that were chosen:
{marbles_chosen}')
```

Pick Marbles!

Once you've reviewed your code, save and run the program.

```
Awesome! You found a green marble. If you would like
another marble, you have 3 pick(s) left.
```

```
Here are all the marbles that were chosen:
['red', 'green']
```

When the program starts, Python first imports the random module so that the `random.choice()` function can be used to pick a random marble from `secret_bag`. Python then starts the first of five loops assuming that `tries_remaining` is greater than 0. Since `tries_remaining` is greater than 0, a random item is selected from `secret_bag` and added to `marbles_chosen`. The value for `tries_remaining` is then decreased by 1. Python then checks to see whether the randomly selected marble is green. If the marble is green, the item is added to `collection` and removed from `secret_bag`. Python confirms whether the randomly selected marble is now in `collection`. If the marble is in `collection`, the loop breaks and prints that a green marble was found in addition to the number of tries remaining. Python continues the loop until one of two conditions is met: `tries_remaining` is not greater than 0 *or* a green marble is selected. Once the loop stops, a list of the items in `marbles_chosen` is printed.

You can add more conditional logic to the program and set your own limitations and rules for picking marbles out of the secret bag! Be sure to watch your indentations as you nest `if` statements. IDLE is pretty helpful in indenting the proper number of spaces!

Here is an example of the full program for `marbles.py`:

```
# Import the random module into the program
import random

# List of marbles in the marble collection
collection = ['red', 'pink', 'orange', 'red', 'pink',
'yellow', 'pink', 'yellow']
```

```python
# List of marbles in the secret bag
secret_bag = ['pink', 'blue', 'green', 'orange', 'red',
'purple', 'green', 'blue', 'blue', 'red', 'green',
'purple', 'yellow', 'red', 'pink', 'red', 'green',
'yellow']

# Empty list of marbles chosen which stores the
randomly selected marbles
marbles_chosen = []

# Number of tries remaining for randomly selecting a
marble
tries_remaining = 5

# For loop used to randomly select marbles 5 times
unless a green marble is chosen.
# For each marble selected, the number of tries
decreases.
for x in range(6):
    if tries_remaining > 0:
        selection = random.choice(secret_bag)
        marbles_chosen.append(selection)
        tries_remaining -= 1
        if selection == 'green':
            collection.append(selection)
            secret_bag.remove(selection)
            if ('green' in collection):
                print(f'Awesome! You found a green
marble. If you would like another marble, you have
{tries_remaining} pick(s) left.')
                break

    else:
        print('Sorry, you are out of tries. Please come
back tomorrow and try again!')

print(f'Here are all the marbles that were chosen:
{marbles_chosen}')
```

10

while Loops

In the previous chapter, you learned how to repeat actions in Python using a `for` loop. However, what should you do if you want your loop to keep repeating while a condition is true? Get ready to learn about Python's other loop, the *while loop*!

Create a while Loop

Suppose you have a variable x that decreases each time a loop is completed. With each decrease, the string "x is greater than 0" is printed until x is equal to the value 0. How would you go about setting this up? You could use a while loop!

while condition:
action1
action2
action3

A while loop repeats (or *iterates*) all actions indented underneath the while loop so long as the condition you define is true. Let's use a while loop to set up the previous logic for the variable x.

```
>>> x = 5
>>> while x > 0:
        print("x is greater than 0")
        x -= 1


x is greater than 0
x is greater than 0
x is greater than 0
x is greater than 0
x is greater than 0
```

In the previous code, the variable x is assigned the value 5. This value is where the while loop starts to count down. Just below the variable assignment, the while loop logic begins with the condition "while x is greater than 0." What this means is that while the value of x is more than 0, the action inside the `while` loop happens. In this case, a string is printed, and the value of x is decreased by 1.

As you can see, the string is printed five times given that x is greater than 0 for five of the loops that are completed. To double-check that the value of x is in fact decreasing *and* greater than 0, modify the code to return the current value of x in the printed string. You can use string formatting with the `f` syntax to insert the current value of x into your string.

```
>>> x = 5
>>> while x > 0:
        print(f"x value is {x}")
        x -= 1


x value is 5
x value is 4
x value is 3
x value is 2
x value is 1
```

break statement

Like `for` loops, you can stop a `while` loop using a *break statement*. A break statement stops the loop from looping even if the condition is true.

while condition1:
action
if condition2:
break

An `if` statement helps the loop determine whether it should break. If the condition in the `if` statement is met, the loop will stop. However, if the condition in the `if` statement hasn't been met, the loop continues until the condition is met. Let's see a break statement in action!

```
>>> num = 2
>>> while num <= 10:
        if num == 8:
            break
        print(num)
        num += 2


2
4
6
```

In the previous code, the variable num is assigned to the value 2. The `while` loop checks whether the value of num is less than or equal to 10. If the condition is true, then the `while` loop checks whether the value of num is equal to 8. If the value of num is equal to 8, then the `while` loop breaks. However, if the value of num is not equal to 8, then the value of num is printed, and the value of num is increased by 2. The `while` loop then loops again and finally breaks once the value of num is 8.

continue statement

Also like `for` loops, you can stop running the code at a point and continue to the next iteration. A continue statement tells the loop to return to the top of the loop at some other point in the code.

while *condition1:*
action1
if *condition2:*
continue
action2

Let's use a continue statement to print every even number from 2 to 10. Define a variable num and assign the value 2. The value of num should increase by 1 after the completion of each loop. If the current value of num is an even number, print num to the console.

```
>>> num = 2
>>> while num <= 10:
        if (num % 2) == 0:
            print(f'{num} is an even number')
        num += 1
        continue

2 is an even number
4 is an even number
6 is an even number
8 is an even number
10 is an even number
```

In the previous code, the while loop checks that the value of num is less than or equal to 10. If the condition is true, then the while loop checks whether the value of num modulo 2 is equal to 0. As a reminder, modulo returns the remainder of two divided numbers. If the remainder of a number divided by 2 is 0, then the number is an even number. As for the previous code, if the remainder of modulo divided by 2 is 0, then the number is an even number. Therefore, the value of num is printed to the console and num is increased by 1. The while loop then continues.

while, else Loops

Suppose you want a block of code to run once the condition for your while loop is no longer true. Including an *else statement* makes this possible!

while condition:
action1
else:
action2

For each iteration, Python checks whether the condition specified in the while loop is true. However, once the condition is false, the action inside the else statement occurs.

Let's give this a try by creating logic for a model rocket launch. Suppose that the model rocket should be launched only if it's not windy. As the while loop counts down from 10 to 1, ask the user whether it's windy. If it's windy, break the loop and print the phrase Mission Aborted. If it's not windy, continue the countdown, launch the model rocket, and print the We Have Liftoff! phrase.

```
>>> countdown = 10
>>> while countdown > 0:
        print(countdown)
        countdown -= 1
        if input('Is it windy? ') == 'yes':
                print('Mission Aborted')
                break
else:
        print('We Have Liftoff!')


10
Is it windy? no
9
Is it windy? no
8
Is it windy? no
7
Is it windy? no
6
Is it windy? no
5
Is it windy? no
4
Is it windy? no
3
Is it windy? no
2
Is it windy? no
1
Is it windy? no
We Have Liftoff!
```

The previous code starts with a variable countdown that is
assigned the value 10. A while loop checks whether the value
of countdown is greater than 0. If the condition is true, the

value of `countdown` is printed and then decreased by 1. Next, a conditional statement uses the `input()` method to ask whether it is windy. If the user's input is equal to the string `yes`, then the phrase `Mission Aborted` is printed, and the `while` loop breaks. However, if the user's input is not equal to the string `yes`, then the `while` loop continues with the next iteration. Once the `while` loop is complete, the `else` statement prints the `We Have Liftoff!` phrase.

 ## Checkpoint

Which of the following statements is true about `while` loops?

A. A `while` loop iterates as long as a specified condition is false. A `while` loop can break by using a break statement. A break statement stops the loop and no longer runs the code inside the `while` loop.

B. A `while` loop iterates only once regardless of whether a specified condition is true or false.

C. A `while` loop iterates as long as a specified condition is true. A `while` loop can break by using a `continue` statement. A `continue` statement stops the loop and no longer runs the code inside the `while` loop.

D. A `while` loop iterates so long as a specified condition is true. A `while` loop can break by using a break statement. A break statement stops the loop and no longer runs the code inside the `while` loop.

Project: Kickball Teams

Description:

Jaleesa and Rahim have been chosen as captains for today's game of kickball. Rather than pick their own teammates one by one, they've chosen to let Python pick the players instead! Using the random module, create a program that randomly assigns players to a team. The program should continue to add players to a team until the total number of players on the team is eight (seven plus the captain). Any players not selected for the first team will automatically be assigned to the second team.

After you create the program, run the program and print the list of players assigned to each team.

The following are the players who are playing in today's game of kickball:

Anastasia

Eli

Jamal

Jada

Theo

Michelle

Adam

Rhea

Charlie

Jasmine

Marley

Kenji

Sydney

Yara

Steps:

Open IDLE

Before you begin to code, open IDLE and create a new file. Save your new file with the filename **kickball.py**.

Import the Random Module

Python comes equipped with built-in modules that you can use in your programs. Such modules enable you to perform some interesting actions in your code! To use a module in Python, you must first import the module.

import module

The *random* module enables you to return random values. Within the random module is a `random.choice()` function that returns a random item from a list. In IDLE, import the random module so that you can use the `random.choice()` function in your program to pick a player at random from a list of available players.

```
import random
```

Create a List for Players

Players will be chosen at random from the list of players playing in today's game of kickball. The program will first randomly select all seven players for Jaleesa's team. Any player not selected for Jaleesa's team will be a player on Rahim's team. Since a player can be chosen only once, the player should be removed from the list of available players when they are selected for Jaleesa's team.

Create a list `available_players` that consists of the 14 available players listed earlier.

```
available_players = ['Anastasia', 'Eli', 'Jamal',
'Jada', 'Theo', 'Michelle', 'Adam', 'Rhea', 'Charlie',
'Jasmine', 'Marley', 'Kenji', 'Sydney', 'Yara']
```

Create a List for Each Team

Each captain needs their own list of players to keep track of who's on their team. First, create a list named **jaleesas_team** for Jaleesa's team. Be sure to include Jaleesa as a player.

```
jaleesas_team = ['Jaleesa']
```

Now, create a list named **rahims_team** for Rahim's team. Be sure to include Rahim as a player.

```
rahims_team = ['Rahim']
```

Add Players to Jaleesa's Team

The program will select a player at random until the total number of players on Jaleesa's team is 8. You can get the total number of players on Jaleesa's team by getting the length (or len) of the list `jaleesas_team`. The `len()` method will provide you with the total number of items in the list.

Create the beginning of a `while` loop that will iterate while the length of Jaleesa's team is less than 8. Remember, Python starts to count at 0 rather than 1.

```
while len(jaleesas_team) < 8:
```

Next you create the code inside the `while` loop to add a player to the team. This is where the `random` module that was imported earlier comes in handy! Inside the `while` loop, create a variable `player_selected` to store the randomly selected player. The `random.choice()` method randomly selects a player from the `available_players` list.

```
while len(jaleesas_team) < 8:
    player_selected = random.choice(available_players)
```

Next, add (or append) that player to Jaleesa's team. The append() method adds a player to the list.

```
while len(jaleesas_team) < 8:
    player_selected = random.choice(available_players)
    jaleesas_team.append(player_selected)
```

Finally, remove the player from the list if they're selected for Jaleesa's team. The remove() method removes the player from the list.

```
while len(jaleesas_team) < 8:
    player_selected = random.choice(available_players)
    jaleesas_team.append(player_selected)
    available_players.remove(player_selected)
```

When the while loop starts, it checks whether the length of the jaleesas_team list is less than 8. If the length is less than 8, a random player is selected from available_players using random.choice(). The selected player is added to the jaleesas_team list and removed from the available_players list. Once the length of the jaleesas_team list is no longer less than 8, the loop stops.

Add Players to Rahim's Team

Now that Jaleesa's team is squared away, add the remaining players in the available_players list to Rahim's team. You can do so using the extend() method.

```
rahims_team.extend(available_players)
```

Print Players on Each Team

After Jaleesa's team is formed, you need to let the captains and the players know who's on which team. First, print the string "Jaleesa's Team" on its own line.

```
print("Jaleesa's Team")
```

Just below the string "Jaleesa's Team", print the list of players from the `jaleesas_team` list. Remember, if you pass a list variable into a `print()` statement, the format of the output will include the brackets, commas, and quotations. To make the list of players read more like a natural list with just commas, use the * symbol and include the character that separates each item (or player) in the list.

```
print("Jaleesa's Team")
print (*jaleesas_team, sep = ", ")
```

Repeat the same for Rahim's team!

```
print("Rahim's Team")
print (*rahims_team, sep = ", ")
```

When the program starts, Python first imports the random module so that the `random.choice()` function can be used to pick a player from `available_players`. Python then starts the first loop assuming that the length of `jaleesas_team` is less than 8. Since `len(jaleesas_team)` is less than 8, a random player is selected from `available_players` and added to `jaleesas_team`. The selected player is then removed from `available_players`. Python then repeats the loop and checks whether `len(jaleesas_team)` is still less than 8. This loop continues until the condition is no longer true. Since the flow of logic in Python happens from top to bottom, the `for` loop runs next and takes each of the remaining players in `available_players` and appends them to `rahims_team`. In the end, Python prints the list of players on each team.

Here is an example of the full program for `kickball.py`:

```python
# Import the random module to pick a random item in the list
import random

# List of players available to choose from for teammates
available_players = ['Anastasia', 'Eli', 'Jamal', 'Jada',
'Theo', 'Michelle', 'Adam',
'Rhea', 'Charlie', 'Jasmine', 'Marley', 'Kenji', 'Sydney',
'Cooper']

# List of each captain's teams
jaleesas_team = ['Jaleesa']

rahims_team = ['Rahim']


# While-loop that iterates until Jaleesa's team has 8
players total
while len(jaleesas_team) < 8:
    player_selected = random.choice(available_players)
    jaleesas_team.append(player_selected)
    available_players.remove(player_selected)


# For-loop that adds the remaining players to Rahim's
team
rahims_team.extend(available_players)

# Prints the players on each team
print("Jaleesa's Team")
print (*jaleesas_team, sep = ", ")

print("Rahim's Team")
print (*rahims_team, sep = ", ")
```

Functions

Programs in Python often repeat the same set of actions defined in a block of code. Rather than rewrite the same block of code repeatedly in your program, create a *function* that you can use anywhere you need.

Create a Function

In Python, every function has a name, which is what you use to call it. Here's the syntax for defining a function:

def function_name( ):
action 1
action 2

All functions start with the keyword def followed by the name of the function and a pair of parentheses. Just below the function is the function body. The function body contains whatever actions you choose to have your function complete.

Here is an example of a hello_world function that prints the string "Hello World":

```
>>> def hello_world():
        print("Hello World")
```

Call a Function

The function in the prior example won't do anything in your program until you call the function. Calling a function tells your code to run the code inside the function body. To call a function, use the function name and include the parentheses. The parentheses specifically say, "Treat the name as a function and call it."

```
>>> hello_world()
Hello World
```

Notice how you don't need to include a `print` statement in the function call. Since the `hello_world()` function includes a `print` statement in the function body, the string inside the function prints whenever the function is called.

It's worth noting that a function can do more than print strings! Essentially, most of the code you've written up to this point can be placed inside a function body.

Return

You can end the run of a function by including a `return` statement in the function body. A `return` statement appears at the end of the actions within the function body and can include an expression. An *expression* is a combination of values, variables, operators, and calls to functions.

$$\textbf{def function\_name( ):}$$
$$\textbf{action 1}$$
$$\textbf{return}$$

If an expression is included with the `return` statement, the expression is evaluated, and the value is returned. Returning a value is useful as it enables you to use the result value of a function in your code. However, if no `return` statement is included at the end of a function, the function returns None.

Let's re-create the `hello_world()` function from the prior example and include a `return` statement at the end of the function body.

```
>>> def hello_world():
        print('Hello World')
        return

>>> hello_world()
Hello World
```

Parameters

Sometimes, you may need to provide data with your function to complete the action inside the function body. The data that you pass into a function is known as a *parameter*.

def function_name(parameter1, parameter2): action

When you call a function that has parameters, you provide values for the parameters inside the parentheses. These values are known as *arguments*. Python takes the arguments and assigns them to the variables named by the parameters. By default functions accept arguments in order and assigns the arguments to the parameters in that order.

Let's create a `good_morning()` function that greets a person using their first and last names.

```
>>> def good_morning(fname, lname):
        print(f'Hello {fname} {lname}')
        return

>>> good_morning('April', 'Speight')
Hello April Speight
```

The good_morning() function has two parameters, fname and lname. Inside the function body, a string prints that includes the arguments used in the function call for the good_morning() function. When the good_morning() function is called, the two arguments you provide in the parentheses appear in the parameter variables fname and lname inside the function. You can then use these variables like any others inside the function body. It's important to know that a function can accept any type of value as an argument, like an int. For example, the following sum() function takes two parameters, a and b, and returns the sum of the two numbers:

```
>>> def sum(a,b):
        return a + b

>>> sum(5,6)
11
```

▶ Checkpoint

The following block of code contains a code snippet that consists of a function `double()`. **The** `double()` **function takes a number and returns twice the number's value. Label each part of the code block.**

```
    1      2
def double(x):

        3
    return x * 2

      4
double(4)
8
```

Default Arguments

A function can also have default arguments, which makes the parameter optional. The function uses the default value unless one is provided when calling the function.

def function_name(parameter = value):
action

A default value is assigned to a parameter when creating a function. When you call a function that has default values, the default value is used. The following is an example of a function `favorite_season`, which has a parameter `season`. The default value for the parameter `season` is `Summer`.

```
>>> def favorite_season(season="Summer"):
        print(f"{season} is my favorite season.")


>>> favorite_season()
Summer is my favorite season.
```

In the previous example, favorite_season() is called without passing a value into the parentheses. As a result, the string Summer is my favorite season. is printed. However, if you were to pass a value in the function call, the value provided is used instead and therefore printed.

```
>>> def favorite_season(season="Summer"):
    print(f'{season} is my favorite season.')


>>> favorite_season('Spring')
Spring is my favorite season.
```

Since the value Spring is passed into the function call, the string Spring is my favorite season. is printed despite having a default value of Summer for the parameter season.

 # Checkpoint

Ricky is having trouble figuring out why his age_in_ dog_years() **function returns the value** 117 **instead of** 91. **What should Ricky do to make sure that** 91 **prints to the console?**

```
>>> def age_in_dog_years(age, dog_years=7):
        return age * dog_years

>>> age_in_dog_years(13, 9)
117
```

A. Change the function call to age_in_dog_years(age=13, 9).

B. Change the function to def age_in_dog_years(age=117, dog_years=7), which assigns a default parameter of 117 for the age parameter in the function.

C. Pass only the argument 13 into the age_in_dog_years() function call.

D. Replace 9 with dog_years=9 in the function call.

Arbitrary Arguments

You can also create a function without knowing how many arguments will be passed into the function. An arbitrary argument is indicated by a * before the parameter name in a function. Arbitrary arguments are often referred to as *args.

def function_name(*args):
action 1
action 2

Consider the following states_traveled() function that returns a string that prints the names of states visited:

```
>>> def states_traveled(*states):
        for state in states:
            print(f'I have traveled to
{state}.')


>>> states_traveled('Vermont', 'Alaska', 'Florida')
I have traveled to Vermont.
I have traveled to Alaska.
I have traveled to Florida.
```

Since the number of states traveled is unknown, the * is placed before the states parameter in the states_traveled() function. When the states_traveled() function is called, three arguments are provided, one for each state traveled. The for loop created in the body of the states_traveled() function prints a string that includes each of the arguments passed into the function call.

Keyword Arguments

You also have the option to pass arguments into a function call without maintaining the default order. If you don't want to depend on ordering, then you can name the arguments. You can name arguments by creating keyword arguments in the function call. Keyword arguments are often referred to as *kwargs.

function_name(keyword 1 = value 1, keyword 2 = value 2)

To create a keyword argument, assign a value to an argument in the function call. The order of the keyword arguments in the function call do not have to match the order of the parameters in the function.

The following gameshow_contestants() function contains three parameters, which reflect the names of the contestants. The print statement inside the function body prints a string that includes the name of each contestant.

```
>>> def gameshow_contestants(contestant_1,
contestant_2, contestant_3):
        print(f"Here are today's contestants:
{contestant_1}, {contestant_2}, {contestant_3}.")
```

```
>>> gameshow_contestants(contestant_2 = 'Lamont',
contestant_1 = 'Pippa', contestant_3 = 'Sven')
Here are today's contestants: Pippa, Lamont, Sven.
```

The name of each contestant is passed into the function call by naming contestant_2 first followed by contestant_1 and finally by contestant_3. Regardless of the order used for the function call, the string printed within the function body maintains its order by first printing contestant_1, followed by contestant_2 and finally contestant_3.

If you were to call the gameshow_contestants() function without using keyword arguments, the function would print the names in the order in which they appear in the function call.

```
>>> gameshow_contestants('Lamont', 'Pippa', 'Sven')
Here are today's contestants: Lamont, Pippa, Sven.
```

Built-in Functions

Although you could create your own functions to use in a program, Python also has dozens of built-in functions! You've used some of the built-in functions already in prior chapters, as shown here:

- print()
- bool()
- float()
- int()

- `input()`
- `len()`
- `range()`
- `slice()`
- `str()`
- `type()`

There are more than 60 built-in functions available in Python. To review all the built-in functions, visit `docs.python.org/3/library/functions.html`.

Project: Customer Service Bot

Tiny Space is a furniture store that specializes in selling furniture for small spaces. The company has one location in addition to a website, which features a customer service chat window that enables customers to chat in real time with someone from the Tiny Space team. When Addison first started Tiny Space, she and her team handled all incoming chat messages from customers as soon as an incoming message was received. However, business has grown from the early days of Tiny Space, and the Tiny Space team can no longer dedicate a significant amount of their day to responding to chat inquiries. Addison began to explore solutions that could minimize the amount of time spent on conversations with customers.

Addison figured that she could add a chat bot to the chat feature on the Tiny Space website to screen incoming chat messages and route customers to the appropriate person on the Tiny Space team if human assistance is needed. For some inquiries, the chat bot should be able to answer a customer's question without the need to have someone from the Tiny Space online team involved. Addison would also like the bot to mimic an actual conversation with a human.

Help the Tiny Space team by creating a program for the Tiny Space website chat bot.

Additional information for how the chat bot should respond to chat messages is provided next.

Greeting

When a customer starts a chat message with Tiny Space, the bot should greet the customer with the phrase *Thanks for contacting Tiny Space!*.

The bot should then collect the customer's name before continuing with the conversation. After the bot collects the customer's name, the bot should respond with the phrase *Thanks, {insert customer's name}!*.

Inquiry Categories

When a customer starts a chat message with Tiny Space, their inquiry typically falls into one of five categories. The Tiny Space team member responsible for providing human assistance after the initial inquiry screening is provided next to their assigned category, as shown here:

- Store Location and Hours
- Order Status: Elliot

- Issue with Order: Chrissa

- Design Services: Ramon

- Other: Trinity

Store Location and Hours is the only inquiry category that does not require a transfer to a human for assistance.

After the chat bot greets the customer, the bot should respond with this message: *Please select from one of the categories below using the numbers 1–5*. The customer should then select an inquiry category from the categories described earlier. If the customer provides an unrecognizable response, the bot should ask the customer to select a category provided and repeat the list of categories.

Store Location and Hours

Tiny Space is located at 2300 Riverdale Lane, Boston, MA 02101. The store is open Monday–Saturday from 10 a.m. to 6 p.m.

After providing a customer with the store's location and hours of operation, the bot should ask the customer *May I help you with anything else?*. If the customer needs additional help, the list of inquiry categories should display again for the customer. However, if the customer does not need any additional help, the bot should end the conversation with the phrase *Thanks for contacting Tiny Space!*. If the customer selects another inquiry category, the bot should continue the conversation with the prompt for the selected category.

Status of Order

If a customer wants to know the status of their order, the bot should respond with the message *Sure, I can help you with that*.

The bot should then collect the following information from the customer:

- Full name on the order

- Order number

Once the information is collected from the customer, the bot should transfer the conversation to the assigned member of the Tiny Space team for assistance and follow up with the message *Awesome! I'm checking the status of the order now*.

Issue with Order

If a customer has an issue with their order, the bot should respond with the message *I'm sorry that you're experiencing issues with your order*. The bot should then collect the following information from the customer:

- Full name on the order

- Order number

- Issue

Once the information is collected from the customer, the bot should transfer the conversation to the assigned member of the Tiny Space team for assistance and follow up with the message *Thanks for providing that information. I'm looking into this now*.

Design Services

If a customer requests Design Services, the bot should transfer the conversation to the assigned member of the Tiny Space team and respond with the message *I can definitely help you out with your design questions! Tell me how I may be of assistance*. The customer's response should be collected.

Other

If a customer selects Other, the bot should transfer the conversation to the assigned member of the Tiny Space team and respond with the message *No problem, please describe to me how I may be of assistance*. The customer's response should be collected.

Steps:

Here are the steps you need to follow to create the customer service bot.

Open IDLE

Before you begin to code, open IDLE and create a new file. Save your new file with the file name `tinyspace.py`.

Create Greeting Function

The chat bot's greeting is the first thing that the bot says to the customer. This greeting can be placed inside a function `greeting()` and called to start the bot.

```
def greeting():
```

Inside the function body, you should greet the customer and ask for their name. You can use the `input()` method to provide a way for the customer to respond with their name. Be sure to convert the customer's response to capitalize the first letter in their name. By doing so, you can ensure that their name is properly formatted when the chat bot says thanks.

```
def greeting():
    name = input('Thanks for contacting Tiny Space! May
I have your name? ').capitalize()
    print(f'Thanks, {name}!')
    return
```

Create Select Category Function

After the chat bot greets the customer, the bot needs to ask the customer to select a category related to their reason for contacting Tiny Space. You can use the `input()` method again to ask the customer to select 1 of the 5 inquiry categories. Since the bot is designed to repeat the list of categories and follow a specific set of actions based on the customer's response more than once throughout the conversation, create a function `select_category` that contains a set of actions to follow based on the category selected.

```
def select_category():
```

Later in the program, you will create functions for each of the inquiry categories. For now, focus on completing the actions within the `select_category()` function.

The chat bot should first ask the customer to select a category from a list of available categories. Assign the customer's response to a variable `category`. In addition, providing a number surrounded by brackets to the left of each category gives the customer a better idea of which number corresponds to which category.

```
def select_category():
    category = input('Please select from one of the
categories below using the numbers
```

1 - 5. [1] Store Hours & Locations [2] Status of Order
[3] Issue with Order [4] Design Services [5] Other ')

You now need to add logic to the select_category()
function body that can be used to direct the bot to the
appropriate inquiry category function. An if statement is
helpful in this scenario as you can compare the customer's
response to determine which inquiry category function should
be run. Create an if statement that compares whether the
response for category is 1, 2, 3, 4, or 5. Keep in mind that the
customer's response is a str and not an int.

```
def select_category():
    category = input('Please select from one of the
categories below using the numbers 1 - 5. [1] Store Hours
& Locations [2] Status of Order [3] Issue with Order [4]
Design Services [5] Other ')

    if category == '1':


    if category == '2':


    if category == '3':


    if category == '4':


    if category == '5':
```

Each if statement needs a function to call if the customer's
response for category matches the inquiry category's
corresponding number. Add a function call to each if statement

that can be used later in the program to create functions for each inquiry category.

```
def select_category():
    category = input('Please select from one of the
categories below using the numbers 1 - 5. [1] Store Hours
& Locations [2] Status of Order [3] Issue with Order [4]
Design Services [5] Other ')

    if category == '1':
        store_location_hours()
        return

    if category == '2':
        order_status()
        return

    if category == '3':
        order_issue()
        return

    if category == '4':
        design_services()
        return

    if category == '5':
        other()
        return
```

Finally, create a final if statement inside the select_category() function body that compares whether the customer's response for category is *not* one of the valid responses. You can compare multiple strings at a time by checking whether the response for category is not in a list of valid strings. If the customer's response is not 1, 2, 3, 4, or 5, then call the select_category() function so that the chat bot can ask the customer once more to select a category.

```
if category not in ['1', '2', '3', '4', '5']:
    select_category()
```

Create Inquiry Category Functions

Each of the inquiry categories needs its own function that can be called depending on the customer's response. Be sure to use the function names created in the previous step.

Start first with the store_location_hours() function. The store's location can be stored in a variable store. The store's hours can be stored in a variable hours. You can then print a string to the customer that includes the store's location and hours together.

```
def store_location_hours():
    location = '2300 Riverdale Lane Boston, MA 02101'
    hours = 'Monday - Saturday from 10AM to 6PM'
    print(f'Tiny Space is located at {location}. The
store is open {hours}.')
```

Next, the chat bot should ask the customer if they have any additional questions by using the input() method. If the customer's response is yes, then the bot should ask the customer to select an inquiry category. However, if the customer's response is no, then the chat bot should end the conversation. To help compare the customer's response to the strings yes or no, convert the customer's response to all lowercase letters.

```
def store_location_hours():
    location = '2300 Riverdale Lane Boston, MA 02101'
    hours = 'Monday - Saturday from 10AM to 6PM'
    print(f'Tiny Space is located at {location}. The
store is open {hours}.')
```

```
    additional_question = input('May I help you with
anything else? [Yes/No] ').lower()
    if additional_question == 'yes':
        select_category()
    elif additional_question == 'no':
        print('Thanks for contacting Tiny Space!')
    return
```

The next function to create is `order_status()`. This function should first instruct the chat bot to inform the customer that the bot can help them. The chat bot should then ask the customer for the full name on the order in addition to the order number. The response for each question can be collected using the `input()` method and stored to a variable.

```
def order_status():
    print('Sure, I can help you with that.')
    full_name = input('May I have the full name on the
order? ')
    order_number = input('May I have the order number? ')
```

After the bot collects the information from the customer, the conversation should be transferred to the assigned individual on the Tiny Space team. Later in the program, you will create a function for each conversation transfer. For now, make a function call to a new function `transfer_Elliot()` that can be called to transfer the conversation to Elliot.

```
def order_status():
    print('Sure, I can help you with that.')
    full_name = input('May I have the full name on the
order? ')
    order_number = input('May I have the order number? ')
    transfer_Elliot()
    return
```

The next function to create is `order_issue()`. This function should first instruct the chat bot to inform the customer that Tiny Space is sorry that the customer is experiencing issues with their order. The chat bot should then ask the customer for the full name on the order in addition to the order number and the issue. The response for each question can be collected using the `input()` method and stored to a variable. Finally, make a function call to `transfer_Chrissa()` that can be called to transfer the conversation to Chrissa.

```
def order_issue():
    print("I'm sorry that you're experiencing issues
with your order.")
    full_name = input('May I have the full name on the
order? ')
    order_number = input('May I have the order number? ')
    issue = ('Could you please describe the issue with
your order? ')
    transfer_Chrissa()
    return
```

The next function to create is `design_services()`. This function should first instruct the chat bot to inform the customer that Tiny Space can help with their design questions. The conversation should then be transferred to Ramon by making a function call to `transfer_Ramon()`.

```
def design_services():
    print('I can definitely help you out with your
design questions!')
    transfer_Ramon()
    return
```

The final category function to create is `other()`. This function should transfer the conversation directly to Trinity by making a function call to `transfer_Trinity()`.

```python
def other():
    transfer_Trinity()
    return
```

Create Transfer Functions

The program is almost complete! All that's left to create are actions for the transfer functions that you added in the previous step. First, start with the `transfer_Elliot()` function. When the chat bot calls `transfer_Elliot()`, the final thing that the bot should say to the customer is they're checking on the status of the order. This helps create a smooth transition from bot to human so that when Elliot is routed the conversation, the customer should still feel that they're talking to the same person.

```python
def transfer_Elliot():
    print("Awesome! I'm checking the status of the
order now.")
    return
```

The `transfer_Chrissa()` function also follows the same logic. The chat bot thanks the customer for providing the information and informs them that they're looking into the order issue.

```python
def transfer_Chrissa():
    print("Thanks for providing that information. I'm
looking into this now.")
    return
```

The `transfer_Ramon()` and `transfer_Trinity()` functions each instruct the chat bot to request a response from the customer once the conversation is transferred to the Tiny Space team member. Use the `input()` method for each function to ask the customer to provide a response.

```python
def transfer_Ramon():
    design_question = input('Tell me how I may be of
assistance. ')
    return

def transfer_Trinity():
    other_inquiry = input('No problem, please describe
to me how I may be of assistance. ')
    return
```

Start the Chat Bot

To start the chat bot, call the `greeting()` function followed by the `select_category()` function.

```python
greeting()
select_category()
```

When the program starts, Python first calls the `greeting()` function followed by the `select_category()` function. The `select_category()` function asks the customer to select from a list of provided categories. If the customer's response is one of the valid responses, then Python calls the corresponding function, and the actions inside the function run. However, if the customer's response is not a valid response, the `select_category()` function is called again, and the actions within the `select_category()` function body start over.

Here is an example of the full program for `tinyspace.py`:

```python
# Greeting

def greeting():
    name = input('Thanks for contacting Tiny Space! May
I have your name? ').capitalize()
    print(f'Thanks, {name}!')
    return


# Inquiry Category

def select_category():
    category = input('Please select from one of the
categories below using the numbers 1 - 5. [1] Store Hours
& Locations [2] Status of Order [3] Issue with Order
[4] Design Services [5] Other ')

    if category == '1':
        store_location_hours()
        return

    if category == '2':
        order_status()
        return

    if category == '3':
        order_issue()
        return

    if category == '4':
        design_services()
        return

    if category == '5':
        other()
        return
```

```python
    if category not in ['1', '2', '3', '4', '5']:
        select_category()

# Category: Store Location & Hours

def store_location_hours():
    location = '2300 Riverdale Lane Boston, MA 02101'
    hours = 'Monday - Saturday from 10AM to 6PM'
    print(f'Tiny Space is located at {location}. The store
is open {hours}.')
    additional_question = input('May I help you with
anything else? [Yes/No] ').lower()
    if additional_question == 'yes':
        select_category()
    elif additional_question == 'no':
        print('Thanks for contacting Tiny Space!')
    return

# Category: Status of Order

def order_status():
    print('Sure, I can help you with that.')
    full_name = input('May I have the full name on the
order? ')
    order_number = input('May I have the order number? ')
    transfer_Elliot()
    return

# Category: Issue with Order

def order_issue():
    print("I'm sorry that you're experiencing issues
with your order.")
    full_name = input('May I have the full name on the
order? ')
```

```python
    order_number = input('May I have the order number? ')
    issue = ('Could you please describe the issue with
your order? ')
    transfer_Chrissa()
    return


# Category: Design Services

def design_services():
    print('I can definitely help you out with your
design questions!')
    transfer_Ramon()
    return


# Category: Other

def other():
    transfer_Trinity()
    return


# Transfers to Tiny Space online team

def transfer_Elliot():
    print("Awesome! I'm checking the status of the
order now.")
    return


def transfer_Chrissa():
    print("Thanks for providing that information. I'm
looking into this now.")
    return


def transfer_Ramon():
    design_question = input('Tell me how I may be of
assistance. ')
    return


def transfer_Trinity():
```

```
    other_inquiry = input('No problem, please describe
to me how I may be of assistance. ')
    return

# Call the functions to start the chat bot

greeting()
select_category()
```

12

Dictionaries

Python is a great choice of languages to use when working with sets of data! You previously learned how to create a list to store items, each of which consists of a singular object. But sometimes, named values may be more appropriate for the data you're using. How can you store named values? This sounds like a job for a *dictionary*!

Create a Dictionary

A *dictionary* is a list of named values, which means that each item in the list consists of a key and a value, often referred to as a *key-value pair*.

dictionary_name = {key: value, key: value}

The collection of data inside a dictionary is surrounded by curly braces, {}. Each item (key-value pair) has the syntax *key*: *value*. Keys must be unique in the dictionary and can be quoted strings, numbers, or tuples. Each key can have any value of any type. The items inside a dictionary are separated by commas. Since dictionaries can be rather lengthy, you can format a dictionary in a manner that's visually easier for you to read.

dictionary_name = {
key: value,
key: value
}

The following are grades for a recent math test. On the left, the name of the student is provided, and on the right, the grade that they received on the test is provided.

Angelo	77%
Samir	93%
Raquel	84%
Louis	62%
Analicia	87%
Tori	95%

Let's create a dictionary called `math_test` to store everyone's test scores.

```
>>> math_test = {
        "Angelo": 77,
        "Samir": 93,
        "Raquel": 84,
        "Louis": 62,
        "Analicia": 87,
        "Tori": 95
        }
>>> print(math_test)
{'Angelo': 77, 'Samir': 93, 'Raquel': 84, 'Louis': 62,
'Analicia': 87, 'Tori': 95}
```

Each student's name and math test grade line is created as a key-value pair. The student's name is surrounded by quotes since their name is a string. However, the test score itself is not surrounded by quotes since the value is an integer. If you print the `math_test` variable, all key-value pairs in the dictionary print to the console.

Dictionaries can be changed, which is great because that gives you the flexibility to modify the key-value pairs stored inside a dictionary! Let's explore ways to modify a dictionary.

Checkpoint

Briana created a dictionary to store her friend's favorite rides at the carnival. When she tries to print the dictionary, she receives the error `SyntaxError: invalid syntax`**. Whose item should Briana change to fix her dictionary so that the dictionary can print without errors?**

```
>>> carnival_rides = {
        "Bryant": "Tilt-a-World",
        "Suzie: "Bananarama Slide",
        "Gary": "Mind Twister",
        "Mandy": "Gloopy Boop"
        }
SyntaxError: invalid syntax
```

A. Change Bryant's item to this: "Bryant" : Tilt-a-World
B. Change Mandy's item to this: Mandy : Gloopy Boop
C. Change Gary's item to this: Gary : "Mind Twister"
D. Change Suzie's item to this: "Suzie" : "Bananarama Slide"

Access Items in a Dictionary

The value of the keys inside a dictionary can be retrieved (or accessed) by referencing the key name.

dictionary_name[key]

Brackets are placed after the dictionary variable name, and the key is placed inside the brackets. You can give this a try with the `math_test` dictionary by accessing the value for Tori's test score.

```
>>> print(math_test["Tori"])
95
```

In the previous example, Tori's test score is accessed from the `math_test` dictionary and printed.

Check Whether a Key Is in a Dictionary

To check whether a key is in a dictionary, create an `if` statement that uses the `in` operator.

if key in dictionary_name:
action

The `in` operator is used to check whether the provided key exists in the dictionary. If the key is found inside the dictionary, Python runs the action inside the `if` statement body.

Using the `math_test` dictionary, you can check whether Samir is in the dictionary.

```
>>> if "Samir" in math_test:
        print("Samir is a key in the dictionary.")


Samir is a key in the dictionary.
```

In the previous example, Python checks whether the string `"Samir"` is a key in the `math_test` dictionary. Since `"Samir"` is a key in the `math_test` dictionary, the string `"Samir is a key in the dictionary. "` prints to the console.

Add a Key-Value Pair to a Dictionary

You can add an additional key-value pair to a dictionary by referencing the key and assigning its value.

dictionary_name[key] = value

The dictionary variable name appears first and is followed by the new key surrounded by brackets. The value for the key is then assigned following the equal sign.

Let's add another student and grade to the `math_test` dictionary. Choose a name of your liking and add a grade for the test score.

```
>>> math_test["Donald"] = 88
>>> print(math_test)
{'Angelo': 77, 'Samir': 93, 'Raquel': 84, 'Louis': 62,
'Analicia': 87, 'Tori': 95, 'Donald': 88}
```

In the previous example, the key `Donald` and the value `88` are added to the dictionary. Now, when you print the dictionary, the new key-value pair displays at the end of the dictionary. Whenever a new key-value pair is added to a dictionary, the pair is added at the end of the dictionary.

If you reference an existing key, you can assign a new value. Let's see this in action by changing Louis' test score from 62 to 72.

```
>>> math_test["Louis"] = 72
>>> print(math_test)
{'Angelo': 77, 'Samir': 93, 'Raquel': 84, 'Louis': 72,
'Analicia': 87, 'Tori': 95, 'Donald': 88}
```

When the `math_test` dictionary prints, Louis' new test score is now in the dictionary.

 ## Checkpoint

Gus maintains a dictionary of books he's read that includes a rating of the book that is on a scale of 1–5.

```
>>> books = {
        "Much Ado About Nothing": 3,
        "Their Eyes Were Watching God": 5,
        "Invisible Man": 4,
        }
```

He recently finished reading *Speak* and would like to rate the book as a 5. Which line of code is the correct way for Gus to add his rating for *Speak* to his dictionary?

A. `books["Speak"] = 5`
B. `[books]["Speak"] = 5`
C. `books["Speak] = 5`
D. `"books" [Speak] = 5`

Remove a Dictionary Item

There are three ways to remove items from a dictionary: `pop()`, `popitem()`, and `del`.

pop() Method

A dictionary's `pop()` method removes an item identified with a given key and returns the item's value.

dictionary_name.pop(key)

You can give this a try by removing Analicia and her test score from the `math_test` dictionary.

```
>>> math_test.pop("Analicia")
87
>>> print(math_test)
{'Angelo': 77, 'Samir': 93, 'Raquel': 84, 'Louis': 72,
'Tori': 95, 'Donald': 88}
```

After the `pop()` method is applied to the `math_test` dictionary, Analicia's value prints to the console. However, if you now print the `math_test` dictionary, Analicia's key-value pair no longer appears in the dictionary.

popitem() Method

A dictionary's `popitem()` method removes the last item in the dictionary and returns that item.

dictionary_name.popitem()

Try `popitem()` on the `math_test` dictionary to see the item at the last index removed.

```
>>> math_test.popitem()
('Donald', 88)
>>> print(math_test)
{'Angelo': 77, 'Samir': 93, 'Raquel': 84, 'Louis': 72,
'Tori': 95}
```

In the `math_test` dictionary, the item `'Donald': 88` is at the last index of the dictionary. After the `popitem()` method is applied to the `math_test` dictionary, Donald and his test score are printed to the console. However, if you now print the `math_test` dictionary, Donald's key-value pair no longer appears in the dictionary.

Loop through Dictionaries

There are several ways to loop through a dictionary using a for loop.

Print All Keys

By default, when you loop through a dictionary, the keys are returned.

```
>>> for student in math_test:
        print(student)
```

```
Angelo
Samir
Louis
Tori
```

In the previous example, the for loop loops through each item (or student) in the dictionary. Each key is then printed one by one on its own line to the console.

You could also print the keys in a dictionary using the keys() method.

for key in dictionary_name.keys( ):
print(keys)

The keys() method is applied to the end of the dictionary variable name. This ensures that Python refers to the keys in the dictionary. Give this a try using the math_test dictionary!

```
>>> for key in math_test.keys():
        print(keys)
```

```
Angelo
```

```
Samir
Louis
Tori
```

Print All Values

Although keys are returned by default, you can also print the values in a dictionary. To do so, reference the dictionary variable name and include the item variable in a pair of brackets.

print(dictionary_name[key])

By passing the `math_test` dictionary and `student` item variable into a `print` statement, you can print each student's test score.

```
>>> for student in math_test:
        print(math_test[student])
```

```
77
93
72
95
```

The test score for each student is printed one by one on its own line to the console. Another way to return all values in a dictionary is to use the `values()` method.

for *item* in dictionary_name.values( ): print(*item*)

The `values()` method is applied to the end of the dictionary variable name. This ensures that Python refers to the values in the dictionary. Give this a try using the `math_test` dictionary!

```
>>> for student in math_test.values():
        print(student)


77
93
72
95
```

Print Keys and Values

Earlier in this chapter, you learned how to print a dictionary. Another way to print the items in a dictionary is by looping through the dictionary using the items() function.

for key, value in dictionary_name.items( ): print(key, value)

The item pair (the key and value) are represented by variables in the for loop. The items() function is applied to the end of the dictionary variable name, which ensures that Python refers to all items in the dictionary.

When applied to the math_test dictionary, the variable student represents the key, and the variable score represents the value. Python prints each key and value together on their own line.

```
>>> for student, score in math_test.items():
        print(student, score)


Angelo 77
Samir 93
Louis 72
Tori 95
```

Checkpoint

Which code snippet could be used to print only the values in the `birthday_month` **dictionary?**

```
>>> birthday_month = {
        "Aya": "June",
        "Clair": "August",
        "Noah": "December"
        }
```

A.

```
>>> for month in birthday_month.values():
        print(month)
```

B.

```
>>> for person in birthday_month:
        print(birthday_month[person])
```

C.

```
>>> for person, month in birthday_month.items():
        print(person)
```

D. A, B, and C

Nested Dictionaries

Dictionaries can also contain many dictionaries! Storing multiple dictionaries inside a dictionary is known as *nesting*.

```
dictionary_name = {
        "nested_dictionary" : {
                key : value,
                key : value
        },
        "nested_dictionary" : {
                key : value,
                key : value
        }
}
```

Each individual dictionary starts with a name for the nested dictionary and is separated by a pair of curly braces, {}.

Let's say that you have a set of grades by subject and grade-point average (GPA) for three students. Using a nested dictionary, you can store everyone's grades for all their subjects into one larger dictionary.

```
>>> gradebook = {
  "Mylene" : {
    "English" : "A",
    "Math" : "A",
    "Science": "B",
    "GPA": 3.7
  },
  "Terrell" : {
    "English" : "C",
    "Math" : "B",
    "Science": "A",
    "GPA": 3.2
  },
```

```
  "Joseph" : {
    "English" : "B",
    "Math" : "B",
    "Science": "B",
    "GPA": 3.0
  }
}
```

If you intend to iterate over each item and produce output, it's best practice to stay consistent with the order of key-value pairs inside each nested dictionary. In doing so, the data inside the nested dictionaries aligns with one another.

You can apply everything learned in this chapter to a nested dictionary—just make sure that you're referring to the correct inner dictionary! Provided next are examples of how to work with the data inside nested dictionaries. Although the examples provided are not a complete list, you can refer to the previous sections of this chapter and apply similar logic to any nested dictionary.

Access Items in a Nested Dictionary

How would you go about accessing an item inside a nested dictionary? If you recall from the previous section on accessing values, you must first reference the dictionary name and then surround the key in brackets. The same rules apply for nested dictionaries!

```
>>> print(gradebook["Mylene"]["English"])
A
```

First provide the name of the dictionary variable and then reference the nested dictionary's name. After you've done that, you can provide the name of the key as well in brackets! In the previous example, the value for Mylene's English grade is printed. You could read the code as follows: the value for `English` that is in the `Mylene` dictionary inside the `gradebook` dictionary.

Add a Key-Value Pair to Nested Dictionary

You can add items to a nested dictionary by referencing the nested dictionary by name and creating a new key and value.

```
>>> gradebook["Mylene"]["Art"] = "A"
>>> print(gradebook["Mylene"])
{'English': 'A', 'Math': 'A', 'Science': 'B', 'GPA':
3.7, 'Art': 'A'}
```

In the previous example, the key `Art` is added to the `Mylene` dictionary. The value provided for `Art` is A.

To change a value in a nested dictionary, first access the item and assign the new value for the key-value pair you'd like to change.

```
>>> gradebook["Mylene"]["English"] = "B"
>>> mylene_english_grade = gradebook["Mylene"]
["English"]
>>> print(mylene_english_grade)
B
```

In this example, the grade (or value) of Mylene's English class is changed from an A to a B.

Remove the Last Item from a Nested Dictionary

To remove the last item from a nested dictionary, apply the pop() method to the end of the reference dictionary.

```
>>> gradebook["Mylene"].pop()
('Art', 'A')
>>> print(gradebook["Mylene"])
{'English': 'B', 'Math': 'A', 'Science': 'B', 'GPA':
3.7}
```

   Since none of the other students has a grade listed for Art, you can remove the new Art item created by applying the pop() method to the end of Mylene's dictionary.

Loop through a Nested Dictionary

Looping through a nested dictionary still requires a variable to represent the item in addition to the name of the dictionary. In the case of the gradebook dictionary, you can loop through the names of the nested dictionaries as follows:

```
>>> for student in gradebook:
        print(student)
```

```
Mylene
Terrell
Joseph
```

   By providing just the name of the larger dictionary gradebook, the name of each nested dictionary is printed to the console. If you want to loop through the items inside each nested dictionary, consider trying one of the options explained earlier in this chapter.

```
>>> for student,grades in gradebook.items():
        print(student,grades)


Mylene {'English': 'B', 'Math': 'A', 'Science': 'B',
'GPA': 3.7}
Terrell {'English': 'C', 'Math': 'B', 'Science': 'A',
'GPA': 3.2}
Joseph {'English': 'B', 'Math': 'B', 'Science': 'B',
'GPA': 3.0}
```

In the previous example, a for loop is created to loop through each item in the nested dictionaries. The complete nested dictionary name, key, and values are printed one by one on their own lines to the console.

Project: School Musical Sign-Ups

It's time for the annual school musical! This year, Vijay is in charge of casting student actors for his newly written musical *A Day Without a Principal*. Auditions are scheduled to happen soon; however, Vijay still needs to create a program that gives those interested in auditioning the ability to sign up for their preferred role. Furthermore, his time is limited for each day of auditions. Vijay can have only five students audition per day. Therefore, the sign-up list will be open to complete on a first-come, first-served basis, whereas after five students signed up, the sign-up list will close. Vijay plans to run the program on multiple days and will therefore need the ability to have the program run when necessary and close after five students sign up.

Vijay needs to complete auditions for these four roles:

- Principal

- Teacher

- Troublemaker

- Students

The program should prompt the student to answer the following questions:

1. What is your name?

2. What is your grade?

3. What is your preferred role?

The responses to each question should be stored inside a dictionary so that Vijay can later look at everyone's information in addition to their preferred role.

Your job is to create such a program so that Vijay can begin the sign-up process for the school musical auditions.

Steps:

Open IDLE

Before you begin to code, open IDLE and create a new file. Save your new file with the file name `auditions.py`.

Create a Dictionary to Store Responses

Let's first create a dictionary to store the student responses to the sign-up questions. To help keep the audition interests organized, use a nested dictionary to store data about which student signed up for each role. For now, leave the items in the dictionary empty.

```
auditions = {
    "Principal" : {
        },
    "Teacher" : {
        },
    "Troublemaker" : {
        },
    "Students" : {
        }
    }
```

In the previous code snippet, `auditions` is the name of the dictionary. Inside the `auditions` dictionary are four nested dictionaries: `Principal`, `Teacher`, `Troublemaker`, and `Students`. Each dictionary is currently empty given that the responses from the students will be added as the program runs.

Ask for Input

Create a variable for the first sign-up question from earlier and use the `input()` function to ask the student for a response. To ensure that the student's name is formatted properly, convert the student's response to capitalize only the first letter in their response.

```
name = input('What is your name? ').capitalize()
```

By applying the `capitalize()` method to the end of the `input()` function, the first letter of the input provided by the student is capitalized.

Next, you need to create a variable for the second sign-up question. To provide guidance on how students should respond, create a question that asks the student to enter a number to reflect their grade.

```
grade = (input('What is your grade? (Please respond
with a number) '))
```

When using a pair of parentheses inside a pair of parentheses, be sure to close each pair; otherwise, an error occurs!

Finally, create a variable for the final sign-up question. Like the prior question about the student's grade, the student should provide a number to reflect which of the four roles interests them.

```
role = input('''What is your preferred role? Please
select a number from the following
options:
                [1] Principal
                [2] Teacher
                [3] Troublemaker
                [4] Student
                ''')
```

Triple quotes enable you to write multiline strings. So long as a string is surrounded by triple quotes, you can place each role in your program on a separate line. When the question prints to the console, each role displays by itself on its own line.

Add a Response to the Nested Dictionary

You now need to provide logic that creates a new item in the appropriate nested dictionary. Depending on which role the student selects to audition, the student's name and grade should create a new key-value pair in the appropriate nested dictionary. For example, if a student selects the role Principal, the responses from their input should create a new key-value pair in the Principal nested dictionary.

Let's start by creating an if statement that checks whether the student is auditioning for the role of Principal. Since input() function responses by default are the type str, the if statement should check whether the response is the string '1' and not the int or float 1.

Inside the if statement, add the student's response for the name and grade variables as key-value pairs to the nested Principal dictionary.

```
if role == '1':
    auditions['Principal'][name] = grade
```

The variable name can be placed into the brackets for the key, whereas the variable grade is assigned to represent the value.

Now, you should check whether the student chose to audition for the role of Teacher. You can apply the same logic as the previous if condition to an elif statement.

```
elif role == '2':
    auditions['Teacher'][name] = grade
```

The elif statement checks whether the response for the role variable is '2'. If the value is '2', then the student's name and grade are added to the nested Teacher dictionary. The same logic can be applied for the role of Troublemaker. Create another elif statement to add sign-ups for the role of Troublemaker.

```
elif role == '3':
    auditions['Troublemaker'][name] = grade
```

Finally, create an `else` statement for the final condition of whether the student is signing up to audition for the role of Students.

```
else:
    auditions['Student'][name] = grade
```

Loop the Sign-Up Form

Currently, if you run the program, the sign-up process occurs only once. Since sign-ups are an ongoing process, the program should run until five students have signed up to audition. This sounds like a job for a `for` loop and a function!

First, place the sign-up process code that you previously created into a function. Be sure to include the variables that were created to store each student's response.

```
def sign_up():
    name = input('What is your name? ').capitalize()
    grade = str(input('What is your grade? (Please
respond with a number) '))
    role = input('''What is your preferred role? Please
select a number from the following options:
                [1] Principal
                [2] Teacher
                [3] Troublemaker
                [4] Student
                ''')

    if role == '1':
        auditions['Principal'][name] = grade
    elif role == '2':
        auditions['Teacher'][name] = grade
    elif role == '3':
        auditions['Troublemaker'][name] = grade
    else:
        auditions['Student'][name] = grade
```

The new `sign_up()` function now includes the entire sign-up process. Now, create a `for` loop outside the `sign_up()` function that loops a total of five times. The `range()` function can be used to tell the loop to iterate whatever number of times that is passed into the function.

```
for i in range(5):
```

Since the loop should iterate five times, the number 5 is passed into `range()`. Finally, inside the `for` loop body, call the `sign_up()` function. Calling the function inside the `for` loop ensures that the sign-up process runs five times.

```
for i in range(5):
    sign_up()
```

Once the loop stops, you should inform students that sign-ups are over for the day. Add a `print` statement to the code that informs students that sign-ups are closed.

```
print("Sign-ups for 'A Day without a Principal' are now
closed")
```

Print the Sign-Ups

After sign-ups are over, a list of everyone signed up to audition should print. Ideally, the printout should be organized by role. Underneath each role, the students and their respective grades should display. You can use another `for` loop to do so!

Let's start by printing a list of everyone signed up to audition for the role of Principal. First, create a `print` statement that reads `Role: Principal`.

```
print("Role: Principal")
```

After the `print` statement, add a `for` loop that iterates through the nested dictionary for Principal and prints each student's name and their grade. You can use the `items()` function to print both the key and the value for an item.

```
for student, grade in auditions['Principal'].items():
    print(student, grade)
```

When the program starts, Python begins the first iteration of the for loop, which calls the `sign_up()` function. The user is asked to respond to three questions. Depending on the user's response for role, the answer for both the user's name and the grade is stored into the appropriate nested dictionary. The loop then iterates again until it has looped for a total of 5 times. After the final loop, Python prints a statement to the console that lets the user know that the sign-up process is closed. Python then follows up with a list of which students signed up for each role.

Here is an example of the full program for `auditions.py`:

```
# Dictionary that stores the audition sign-ups
auditions = {
    "Principal" : {
        },
    "Teacher" : {
        },
    "Troublemaker" : {
        },
    "Student" : {
        }
    }

# Function for the sign-up process
def sign_up():
    name = input('What is your name? ').capitalize()
    grade = str(input('What is your grade? (Please
respond with a number) '))
```

```python
    role = input('''What is your preferred role? Please
select a number from the following options:
                [1] Principal
                [2] Teacher
                [3] Troublemaker
                [4] Student
                ''')

    if role == '1':
        auditions['Principal'][name] = grade
    elif role == '2':
        auditions['Teacher'][name] = grade
    elif role == '3':
        auditions['Troublemaker'][name] = grade
    else:
        auditions['Student'][name] = grade
# For-loop that calls the sign_up() function 12 times
for i in range(5):
    sign_up()

# Printout for the list of students signed up to
audition
print("Sign-ups for 'A Day without a Principal' are now
closed")

print("Role: Principal")
for student, grade in auditions['Principal'].items():
    print(student, grade)

print("Role: Teacher")
for student, grade in auditions['Teacher'].items():
    print(student, grade)

print("Role: Troublemaker")
for student, grade in auditions['Troublemaker'].items():
    print(student, grade)

print("Role: Students")
for student, grade in auditions['Students'].items():
    print(student, grade)
```

Modules

So far in this book you have been writing all your code in a single Python file (with the `.py` extension). With Python, you can put your code, specifically functions and variables, in any number of `.py` files, creating what are called *modules*.

What Is a Module?

A *module* is a file containing a set of functions that you want to include in your program. Rather than re-create the same function or variable across various Python programs, you could store the function or variable inside a module and import that module into multiple Python programs. Modules also help provide organization for Python programs. Instead of having all the code in one file, you can group pieces of the code together in separate modules—like how a book organizes information into chapters. Modules make functions even *more* reusable by enabling you to import a module from a file outside the file in which you are writing a Python program. Although modules can be imported into a program, a module itself is not a program.

Create a Module

You create a module by saving the code you write in a file with a `.py` extension. As a reminder, the `.py` extension is the extension for Python files. The file itself can contain functions as well as variables.

Let's create your first module that will be reused throughout this chapter! The module consists of functions and variables that are used to provide information about the planets in the solar system.

In IDLE, create a new file and save the file as **solarsystem. py**. Inside the `solarsystem.py` file, create a nested dictionary named **planets** that contains an empty dictionary for each planet in the solar system.

```
planets = {
    "Mercury" : {
        },
    "Venus" : {
        },
    "Earth" : {
        },
    "Mars" : {
        },
    "Jupiter" : {
        },
    "Saturn" : {
        },
    "Uranus" : {
        },
    "Neptune" : {
        }
    }
```

If you were to run the solarsystem.py file, the module would do nothing more than define the variable planets.

>Checkpoint

Which file extension is used to create a Python module?

A. python

B. py

C. png

D. html

Let's now add some facts about each planet to the `planets` dictionary. The Planet Facts table contains information that should be added to each planet in the `planets` dictionary.

Planet	Length of Year (Earth days)	Planet Type	Distance From the Sun (astronomical units)
Mercury	88	Terrestrial	0.4
Venus	225	Terrestrial	0.7
Earth	365	Terrestrial	1
Mars	687	Terrestrial	1.5
Jupiter	4333	Gas Giant	5.2
Saturn	10759	Gas Giant	9.5
Uranus	30687	Ice Giant	19.8
Neptune	60190	Ice Giant	30

Use the information in the Planet Facts table to create key-value pairs for each planet.

```
planets = {
    "Mercury" : {
        "length of year": 88,
        "planet type": "Terrestrial",
        "distance from sun": 0.4
        },
    "Venus" : {
        "length of year": 225,
        "planet type": "Terrestrial",
        "distance from sun": 0.7
        },
    "Earth" : {
        "length of year": 365,
        "planet type": "Terrestrial",
        "distance from sun": 1
        },
```

```
    "Mars" : {
        "length of year": 687,
        "planet type": "Terrestrial",
        "distance from sun": 1.5
    },
    "Jupiter" : {
        "length of year": 4333,
        "planet type": "Gas Giant",
        "distance from sun": 5.2
    },
    "Saturn" : {
        "length of year": 10759,
        "planet type": "Gas Giant",
        "distance from sun": 9.5
    },
    "Uranus" : {
        "length of year": 30687,
        "planet type": "Ice Giant",
        "distance from sun": 19.8
    },
    "Neptune" : {
        "length of year": 60190,
        "planet type": "Ice Giant",
        "distance from sun": 30
    }
}
```

We could use the data within the `planets` dictionary to calculate someone's age on a planet. Such a calculation is best stored in a function. Before we create the function, consider which values are needed to calculate someone's age on the planet.

To calculate someone's age on a planet, you need to first multiply their Earth age in years by the total number of days on Earth. This number reflects the age of the person in Earth days. Next, divide the age in Earth days by the length of a year in Earth days on the planet. For example, to calculate the age of a

12-year-old on Mercury, the calculation would look as such: (12 × 365) / 88 = 49.77272727272727.

In the prior example, a person's age, their number of days on Earth, and the length of a year in Earth days for a planet are all values required to calculate someone's age on a planet. However, only the number of days on Earth is a constant, which means the value never changes. Therefore, we could create a variable outside the function to store the value of EARTH_DAYS, which is 365 days. In Python, constants' variable names are written in all capitalized letters.

```
EARTH_DAYS = 365
```

Next, consider which values should be parameters in the function call. We could have the user pass in both their age and the name of a planet.

```
def age_on_planet(age, planet):
```

Within the function body, we can store the calculation value inside a variable called new_age.

```
def age_on_planet(age, planet):
    new_age =
```

The calculation itself first multiplies the user's age and total number of days on Earth. We created an EARTH_DAYS variable outside the function, which can be used to complete this calculation.

```
def age_on_planet(age, planet):
    new_age = (age * EARTH_DAYS)
```

Next, we need to divide the first calculation by the length of a year in Earth days for a given planet. This value is stored in the `planets` dictionary as the key `length of year`. In the new_age calculation, access the key for the `planet` that is passed into the function call.

```
>>> def age_on_planet(age, planet):
        new_age = (age * EARTH_DAYS) / planets[planet]
        ["length of year"]
```

Let's now return the value of new_age as a whole number. You can do so using the `round()` method.

```
def age_on_planet(age, planet):
    new_age = (age * EARTH_DAYS) / planets[planet]
      ["length of year"]
    return round(new_age)
```

Before you finish up with the module for `solarsystem.py`, test the function to ensure that the calculation is set up properly. Be sure to save the `solarsystem.py` file before running the module in IDLE. You can use the prior example of calculating the age of a 12-year-old on Mercury. The age of the person is first passed into the function call followed by the name of the planet.

```
age_on_planet(12, "Mercury")
Result: 50
```

Now that you have confirmed that the function works properly, remove or comment out the function call and save the `solarsystem.py` file. Here is an example of the full module:

```python
# Facts about each planet

planets = {
    "Mercury" : {
        "length of year": 88,
        "planet type": "Terrestrial",
        "distance from sun": 0.4
        },
    "Venus" : {
        "length of year": 225,
        "planet type": "Terrestrial",
        "distance from sun": 0.7
        },
    "Earth" : {
        "length of year": 365,
        "planet type": "Terrestrial",
        "distance from sun": 1
        },
    "Mars" : {
        "length of year": 687,
        "planet type": "Terrestrial",
        "distance from sun": 1.5
        },
    "Jupiter" : {
        "length of year": 4333,
        "planet type": "Gas Giant",
        "distance from sun": 5.2
        },
    "Saturn" : {
        "length of year": 10759,
        "planet type": "Gas Giant",
        "distance from sun": 9.5
        },
```

```
        "Uranus" : {
            "length of year": 30687,
            "planet type": "Ice Giant",
            "distance from sun": 19.8
            },
        "Neptune" : {
            "length of year": 60190,
            "planet type": "Ice Giant",
            "distance from sun": 30
            }
        }

    EARTH_DAYS = 365

    # Calculate the age of a person on a planet

    def age_on_planet(age, planet):
        new_age = (age * EARTH_DAYS) / planets[planet]
          ["length of year"]
        return round(new_age)
```

Use a Module

To use a module, you must first import the module into your program.

import module

To import a module, use an `import` statement followed by the name of the module. The name of the module is the name of the `.py` file, *without* the `.py` extension, that contains the functions and variables to be imported. Make sure to *never* include `.py` in the import statement.

Let's import the `solarsystem` module to access the module's function and variables. In IDLE, run the `solarsystem.py` module. In the new interpreter window that appears, use an `import` statement to import the `solarsystem` module.

```
import solarsystem
```

Now that the `solarsystem` module is imported, you're all set and ready to use the module! Let's start by accessing variables from the `solarsystem` module. The syntax to access a variable from a module is as such:

module.variable

The module name is first used followed by a period and the variable name. In IDLE, access the EARTH_DAYS variable value from the `solarsystem` module.

```
solarsystem.EARTH_DAYS
Result: 365
```

You may notice that after you type the period, IDLE provides you with a list of the dictionary, variable, and function within the `solarsystem` module. This is a helpful feature that can help you keep track of what is available inside the module. If you click the EARTH_DAYS variable, the variable is placed into the line of code.

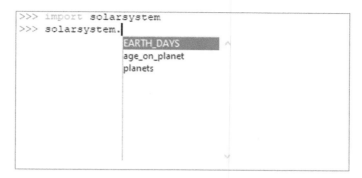

Let's access one of the nested dictionary items within the planets dictionary variable from the solarsystem module. In IDLE, access the "distance from sun" value for Saturn.

```
solarsystem.planets["Saturn"]["distance from sun"]
Result: 9.5
```

Accessing a nested dictionary item within a module follows the same syntax for accessing nested items as introduced in Chapter 12, "Dictionaries."

Let's now use the age_on_planet() function within the solarsystem module. Using a function from a module follows this syntax:

module.function(argument1, argument2)

When using a function from an imported module, IDLE provides documentation for the parameters. You can see this in action when you access the age_on_planet() function from the solarsystem module.

```
>>> import solarsystem
>>> solarsystem.age_on_planet(
                              (age, planet)
```

In IDLE, use the `age_on_planet()` function to calculate a 12-year-old's age on Mars.

```
solarsystem.age_on_planet(12, "Mars")
Result: 6
```

When you call the `age_on_planet` function, the parameters for the function are passed into the parentheses. An `int` value for age is first passed into the argument followed by a `str` value for `planet`.

To use a module in a program file, the module's file must be saved in the same folder on your computer. To try this, create a new file in IDLE called `program.py` and save the program in the same folder as the `solarsystem.py` file. In the `program.py` file, import the `solarsystem` module using an `import` statement.

```
import solarsystem
```

You can follow the same steps previously reviewed to access the dictionary, variable, and function inside the `solarsystem` module. For example, to access the value for the EARTH_DAYS variable, write a `print` statement in the `program.py` file that accesses the EARTH_DAYS variable from the `solarsystem` module.

```
print(solarsystem.EARTH_DAYS)
```

When you run the `program.py` module, the value 365 is printed in a new interpreter window.

 Checkpoint

> **Which of the following is the proper syntax for importing a module named** orderpizza **into a Python program?**
>
> **A.** `orderpizza import`
> **B.** `import module orderpizza`
> **C.** `import orderpizza`
> **D.** `import orderpizza module`

Use an Alias for a Module

An *alias* enables you to refer to a module as a different name. This can be helpful if you have imported a module that has a rather long name. In Python, you create an alias for a module using the as keyword.

import module as alias

When using an alias for a module, be sure to use the alias throughout the entire program. After an alias is created for a module, Python only recognizes the alias name for the module and not the actual name of the module.

You can shorten the name for the `solarsystem` module by creating an alias of `sol`. Let's modify the `program.py` file by importing the `solarsystem` module and creating an alias `sol`.

```
import solarsystem as sol
```

You can access the functions and variables within the `solarsystem` module in the same manner as before; however, this time refer to the module as `sol`. Call the `age_on_planet()` function to calculate the age of a 12-year-old on Venus.

```
print(sol.age_on_planet(12, "Venus"))
```

from Keyword

Oftentimes, you may only need to import specific functions, variables, dictionaries, etc., from a module. You can do so using the `from` keyword.

from *module* import *part*

The `solarsystem` module contains one dictionary, one constant variable, and one function. Modify the `program.py` file to import only the `planets` dictionary.

```
from solarsystem import planets
```

Importing only a part of a module eliminates the need to include the module name to access a variable within the module. For example, to access the `planet_type` value for

Venus, follow the same syntax used for accessing items in nested dictionaries.

```
print(planets["Venus"]["planet type"])
Result: Terrestrial
```

What happens if you try to use the age_on_planet function?

```
age_on_planet(12, "Venus")
Result:
Traceback (most recent call last):
  File "C:/Users/aprilspeight/solarsystem/program.py",
    line 5, in <module>
    age_on_planet(12, "Venus")
NameError: name 'age_on_planet' is not defined
```

Python doesn't recognize the function! Since age_of_ planet() was never imported into program.py, Python is unaware of its existence.

Just as you could create an alias for a module name, you could create an alias for what you import. For example, the alias p can be used for the planets dictionary. In the program. py file, modify the import statement to import planets with the alias p.

```
from solarsystem import planets as p
```

Like before, you can access the planet_type value for Venus without including the solarsystem module name. However, instead of writing the full dictionary name planets, use the alias p.

```
print(p["Venus"]["planet type"])
Terrestrial
```

> Checkpoint

Shannon created a module chessboardgame **that contains functions and variables for programming a computer to play a game of chess. She wants to use the module in a program but would rather give the module name an alias to avoid typing the full module name each time she wants to use part of the module. What is the proper syntax for Shannon to use to refer to the** chessboardgame **module as** chess **when she imports** chessboardgame **into her program?**

A. import chessboardgame as chess
B. chessboardgame import chess
C. import module chessboardgame as chess
D. as chess import chessboardgame

View All Functions in a Module

To get a list of all function names and variable names within a module, you can use the dir( ) function.

dir(module)

The dir() function returns a list of names of all attributes within the module. You can think of the attributes as the features of a module.

In the program file, modify the import statement so that all parts of the solarsystem module are imported into the program. Next, use the dir() function to get all the attributes for the solarsystem module.

```
import solarsystem
```

```
print(dir(solarsystem))
Result: ['__builtins__', '__cached__', '__doc__',
'__file__', '__loader__', '__name__', '__package__',
'__spec__', 'age_on_planet', 'planets']
```

You may notice some attributes that you've never heard of before. Python automatically generates these attributes for you.

- __builtins__ contains a list of all the built-in attributes that can be used within the module. These built-in attributes are automatically added by Python.

- __cached__ tells you the name and location of the cached file that is associated with the module. The cache file speeds up how long it takes to load the Python module.

- __doc__ provides help information for the module. If you create a docstring inside a module, the text within the docstring can be accessed using the __doc__ attribute.

- __file__ tells you the name and location of the module.

- __loader__ provides the loader information for the module. A *loader* is a piece of software that retrieves the module and places it into memory so that Python can use the module.

- __name__ tells you the name of the module.

- __package__ is used by the import system to make it easier to load and manage modules.

- __spec__ contains the specification for importing the module.

Toward the end of the list are the module's attributes that are created by the user. For example, the solarsystem module contains an age_on_planet attribute and a planets attribute.

14

Next Steps

Everything you have learned up to this point has provided you with a foundation for basic Python concepts. So, what is next? Before you move forward with creating your own Python programs, discover additional tools available to help you create and manage your Python projects!

Python Libraries

Modules provide you with the ability to do more with Python by importing modules created by other Python programmers. The website PyPI.org provides what are known as *packages* available for you to install and import into your personal programs. A *package* is a collection of Python modules.

When using packages from the Python community, you must first install the package using PIP. *PIP* is a package manager for Python packages. You can check whether PIP is installed on your computer by typing the command `pip --version` into the terminal. If PIP is not installed, you can download and install it from `pypi.org/project/pip`.

If PIP is installed on your computer, you can install a package using the command `pip install package`. Replace `package` with the name of the package to be installed (for example, `pip install emoji`). To use the functions and variables within a package, follow the same steps introduced in Chapter 13, "Modules."

Let's try the library Matplotlib! Matplotlib is a library for creating static, animated, and interactive visualizations in Python. We'll create a line plot of a few coordinates on a line. You can view documentation for Matplotlib by visiting `matplotlib.org`.

Before using Matplotlib, open a terminal and enter the command **pip install matplotlib**. This command installs the Matplotlib library onto your computer for use in a Python program.

In IDLE, create a new file and save the file as `pyplot.py`. Next, you'll need to import `matplotlib.pylot` to access the functions to create a line plot. Open IDLE and type **import matplotlib.pylot as plt**. Using an alias is helpful here as you can refer to the library with a shorter name, `plt`.

```
import matplotlib.pyplot as plt
```

The `plot()` function included with `matplotlib.pyplot` can be used to plot points on the x- and y-axes. When using the `plot()` function, pass a list of numbers to be plotted on the x- and y-axes into the parentheses. Pass a list of values for the x-axis first followed by another list for the y-axis. In this example, we'll use the following coordinates:

- (1, 2)

- (2, 4)

- (3, 6)

- (4, 8)

In the `pyplot.py` file, use the `plt` alias and the `plot()` function to plot the coordinates.

```
plt.plot([1, 2, 3, 4], [2, 4, 6, 8])
```

Providing labels for the x- and y-axes is helpful to inform what the values on a chart represent. Matplotlib.pylot contains `xlabel()` and `ylabel()` functions, which enable you to provide a label for each axis. The name of the label is passed as a string into the parentheses of the function. We'll label each axis `x-axis` and `y-axis`.

```
plt.xlabel('x-axis')
plt.ylabel('y-axis')
```

The final function we'll use in the pyplot.py program is show(). The show() function displays the chart.

```
plt.show()
```

Save the pyplot.py program and run it. In the new interpreter window that appears, wait a moment for IDLE to display the chart.

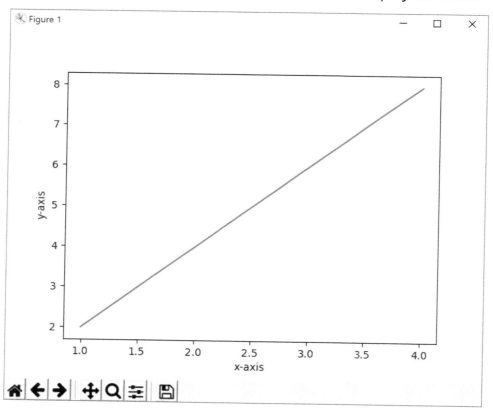

The default visualization plots the coordinates on a line. However, you could style how plots are visualized by modifying the arguments in the plot() function. For example, you can add markers to the chart to display where the coordinates are plotted on the chart with color. In IDLE, modify the `plot()` arguments to include the parameter `'ob'`, which provides a blue circle for each coordinate.

```python
import matplotlib.pyplot as plt

plt.plot([1, 2, 3, 4], [2, 4, 6, 8], 'ob')
plt.xlabel('x-axis')
plt.ylabel('y-axis')
plt.show()
```

Save the `pyplot.py` program and run it. In the new interpreter window that appears, wait a moment for IDLE to display the chart.

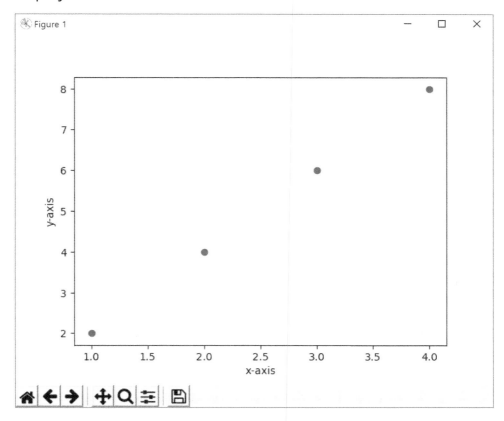

Virtual Environments

As you continue your Python journey, you'll find yourself installing a bunch of libraries for different projects. However, maybe it would be a good idea to keep those separate. Up to this point, you've been using the global Python environment, which is an environment shared between all projects and programs. As you create more programs, it's helpful to keep their environments separate, specifically to have each project maintain its own list of required libraries. Such requirements are referred to as *dependencies*.

With Python, you could use a virtual environment for each of your projects. A virtual environment provides an isolated environment for Python projects. Virtual environments are independent of each other, which means that project dependencies will not conflict with one another.

The package `virtualenv` is used to create a virtual environment. Therefore, the command line is required to create the isolated environment. The command `pip install virtualenv` is used to install the package. After the package is installed, the command `python3 -m venv` is used to create the virtual environment.

The `python3 -m venv <folder name>` command creates a new folder in your current folder that stores all the virtual environment files. In the command, replace `<folder name>` at the end of the command with a folder name of your choice (for example, `python3 -m venv env` creates a folder named env). The virtual environment uses the current version of Python installed on your PATH.

You can choose which version of Python to use with the virtual environment by changing `python3` to the appropriate version (for example, `python3.8` for Python 3.8).

Virtual environments must be activated before use. Depending on your operating system, the file used to activate the virtual environment is stored in either the bin (Windows) or Scripts (iOS, Linux) folder. For Windows, you can activate a virtual environment using the Command Prompt app or PowerShell. The command to activate using the Command Prompt app is `<environment_name>\Scripts\activate.bat`. The command to activate using PowerShell is `<environment_name>\Scripts\Activate.ps1`. For iOS or Linux, you can activate a virtual environment using bash/zsh. The command to activate using bash/zsh is `source <environment_name>/bin/activate`.

Once the virtual environment is activated, you can see the name of the virtual environment at the start of the terminal prompt in parentheses. Any package that you install while the virtual environment is activated is stored inside the virtual environment. When you are done using the virtual environment, enter the command `deactivate` into the terminal.

What happens if you want to share your program with a friend? How would they know what libraries the program exactly needs? You can keep a list of required libraries in a `requirements.txt` file and share that with the program. The person who receives the program can install the requirements into a virtual environment with the command `pip install -r requirements.txt`.

You can learn more about virtual environments by visiting `docs.python.org/3/library/venv.html`.

Integrated Development Environments

Up to this point, you have used IDLE to create and run your Python programs. Although you could use IDLE to create and manage your Python programs, IDLE is not recommended for larger projects. There are other integrated development environments (IDEs) available with additional capabilities to help you create and manage your programs.

An IDE provides you with the ability to edit, run, and fix problems with your Python programs. IDEs provide syntax highlighting and autocomplete to help you out as you code. You can also find and fix errors in your code with the help of an IDE.

Some popular IDEs available to use with Python include PyCharm (`jetbrains.com/pycharm`), Visual Studio Code (`code.visualstudio.com`), and Atom (`atom.io`).

Appendix
Checkpoint Answers

Chapter 4

Which of the following variable names cannot be used in Python?
Answer: B

Naomi wants to print the value of the `movie_title` variable; however, the value assigned needs to be fixed. Which option correctly assigns the movie title *Toy Story 4* to the variable `movie_title`?
Answer: C

When Naomi tries to print the `description` variable, she gets an error. What is wrong with the `description` variable?
Answer: D

If Harrison prints the `current_location` variable, which location will be printed?
Answer: A

Chapter 5

$(2 \times 3) + 7^2$
Answer: 55

72 / 8
Answer: 9.0

$3^3 / 2 + 3^2$
Answer: 22.5

$(5 + 10) + (9 \times 5) - 12$
Answer: 48

Chapter 6

Javier put together a list of his 50 favorite songs of all time. However, he copied and pasted the titles from the internet, which resulted in various title formats. Some titles are in all caps, while some are all lowercase. Javier wants to reformat the list so that the first letter in each word of the song is capitalized. Which string method should Javier use?
Answer: D

Chapter 8

Jared wants to create a list of his favorite superheroes. Which list demonstrates the proper syntax for his list?
Answer: C

What is the item at index [-2] in the list books?
Answer: D

Claudia's list looks to be a bit too long. Which function can she use to get the length of her list?
Answer: A

Since Claudia's list is too long, she needs to remove an item from the list presents. She has decided to remove the basketball since she already has one from her last birthday. Which function can Claudia use to remove the item she no longer wants?
Answer: C

Claudia wants to be specific about the type of camera that she wants for her birthday. Rather than list `camera`, she wants to specify that she wants a Polaroid camera. Which function can Claudia use to change the item `camera` to `Polaroid camera`?
Answer: B

Raul's dog recently had puppies! Before the puppies were born, he decided to let his friends adopt the puppies on a first-come first-serve basis. Prior to the puppies' birth, Raul created a list to collect the names of his friends who were interested in adopting a puppy. Now that the puppies are born, Raul realizes that there are 12 people on the list and only 7 puppies. Print a list of the friends in `adoption_interest` who will be able to adopt a puppy.
Answer: D

Chapter 9

There was a glitch in the grading system that decreased the recent test scores stored in Mr. Klein's grade book by three points. Which `for` loop can Mr. Klein use to increase each test score by three points and print the new test score?
Answer: B

Chapter 10

Which of the following statements is true about `while` loops?
Answer: D

Chapter 11

The following block of code contains a code snippet that consists of a function `double()`. The `double()` function takes a number and returns twice the number's value. Label each part of the code block.

Answer: 1. Function name, 2. Parameter, 3. Variable, 4. Argument

Ricky is having trouble figuring out why his `age_in_dog_years()` function returns the value 117 instead of 91. What should Ricky do to make sure that 91 prints to the console?

Answer: C

Chapter 12

Briana created a dictionary to store her friend's favorite rides at the carnival. When she tries to print the dictionary, she receives the error `SyntaxError: invalidsyntax`. Whose item should Briana change to fix her dictionary so that the dictionary can print without errors?

Answer: D

He recently finished reading *Speak* and would like to rate the book as a 5. Which line of code is the correct way for Gus to add his rating for *Speak* to his dictionary?

Answer: A

Which code snippet could be used to print only the values in the `birthday_month` dictionary?

Answers: D

Chapter 13

Which file extension is used to create a Python module?

Answer: B

Which of the following is the proper syntax for importing a module named orderpizza into a Python program?

Answer: C

Shannon created a module chessboardgame that contains functions and variables for programming a computer to play a game of chess. She wants to use the module in a program but would rather give the module name an alias to avoid typing the full module name each time she wants to use part of the module. What is the proper syntax for Shannon to use to refer to the chessboardgame module as chess when she imports chessboardgame into her program?

Answer: A

Index